Creole Echoes

"*Creole Echoes* makes an important contribution to both American studies and French and Francophone studies by highlighting a significant body of American literature written not in English, but in French. In so doing, this collection draws attention to French as not only a European language, but an American one as well. Containing a total of 108 poems by 33 poets presented in alphabetical order, *Creole Echoes* makes available for an English-speaking audience, for the first time in most cases, a bilingual collection of poems in the French original with translations by Norman R. Shapiro. In an important departure from most other collections, poems by French immigrants to Louisiana, white Creoles, and Creoles of color are included in *Creole Echoes* side by side, which gives full meaning to the term Creole as a non-racially specific term for anyone born of the New World as opposed to the Old."

—Jarrod Hayes, University of Michigan

TRANSLATED BY
Norman R. Shapiro

INTRODUCTION AND NOTES BY
M. Lynn Weiss

FOREWORD BY
Werner Sollors

New Orleans, LA

Creole
Echoes

*The Francophone Poetry
of Nineteenth-Century Louisiana*

SECOND LINE PRESS

Creole Echoes: the francophone poetry of nineteenth-century Louisiana /
translated by Norman R. Shapiro; introduction and notes by M. Lynn
Weiss; foreword by Werner Sollors. English translation © 2004, 2016
Norman R. Shapiro. Arrangement © 2016 Second Line Press. All rights
reserved.

Original publication of this book was supported by grants from the
Louisiana Historical Society; the Thomas and Catharine McMahon
Fund of Wesleyan University, established through the generosity of the
late Joseph McMahon; the College of William and Mary; and Wesleyan
University.

Second Line Press is an imprint of Commonwealth Books, Inc.,
Boston, MA. Distributed to the trade by NBN (National Book Network)
throughout North America, Canada, and the U.K. All Second Line
Press books are printed on acid-free paper, and glued into bindings.
Second Line Press and its logo are registered trademarks of Common-
wealth Books, Inc.

Joseph S. Phillips and Susan J. Wood, Ph.D., Publishers
www.secondlinepress.com

Design & production: Kerrie Kemperman

Frontispiece: *The city of New Orleans and the Mississippi River; Lake
Pontchartrain in distance. Currier & Ives, c. 1885.*

ISBN-13: 978-0-9889627-6-7

Printed in the United States
10 9 8 7 6 5 4 3 2

à Michel Fabre,
avec notre profonde gratitude

Contents

Werner Sollors

Foreword

This eye-opening book, *Creole Echoes: The Francophone Poetry of Nineteenth-Century Louisiana,* makes available an amazingly rich collection of Louisiana poetry, both in the original French and in new English-language translations by Norman Shapiro. The in-depth introduction by Lynn Weiss provides an excellent orientation for readers unfamiliar with the francophone literary tradition in what is now the United States. Indeed, even many professional readers are not yet sufficiently familiar with this vast body of writing from the late eighteenth to the early twentieth century, for it has tended to be marginalized in both American and French literary studies.

This marginalization to some extent emerged as a logical consequence of the writers' "Creole" status, for this position defied an easy *national* location in an age in which literary history was imagined foremost to be the history of national literatures; it was furthermore a *racially ambiguous* term in an era in which the color line was drawn more and more sharply. No wonder the word *Creole* was often the subject of debate, adopted or rejected by countless authoritative-sounding commentators who conferred it on or withheld it from residents of the New World. Johann Friedrich Blumenbach thought the "word originated with the Ethiopian slaves transported in the sixteenth century to the mines in America, who first of all called their own children who were born there, Criollos and Criollas." Balzac associated *Creole* primarily with the mixture of Europe, the tropics, and the Indies. Mme Reybaud thought a fresh and animated pallor characterized the Creole woman, whereas Whitman found the racial ambiguity of such a woman fascinating: was she a European-descended brunette, or was her hue of African blood? Mayne Reid emphatically stated that the "true Creole is not of mixed race" and wrote that "French 'Creole' and the Spanish 'Criollo' bear respectively the same sort of relationship to a Frenchman and a Spaniard that a Yankee bears to an Englishman." Eugène Sue described the white Creole as excessively race-conscious and ready to police racial boundaries. Some observers, such as the novelist Joseph Holt Ingraham, tried to limit the designation to those with French origins because they felt it had been adopted by too many people; others, such as Wilhelm von Humboldt, reported that the Creoles preferred to be called "Americans." It is no wonder that contemporary scholarly definitions are broad. José Juan Arrom, for example, finds that "if all those of European origin born in America are Creoles, not all Creoles are necessarily of pure European origins." And the *Encyclopedia of Southern Culture* lets Gary B. Mills put it philosophically: "A Creole can be anyone who says he is one." The definition operating in this collection is more focused, as it includes only Louisiana residents of European, African, and Caribbean origin who wrote in the French language.

The "echoes" collected here are expressions of the cultural and linguistic Creole community whose writers, as Lynn Weiss explains, "created an indigenous American literature in French." Culled from journals such as *L'Album littéraire* and books such as *Les Cenelles,* the first African-American literary anthology, *Creole Echoes* brings together the best poetry by outstanding writers who often drew on French forms but at times infused them with Louisiana themes. They produced an impressive variety of highly accomplished verse: poems of love and of history, of nightmares and of savannas; melancholy adaptations of Heinrich Heine and political panegyric addressed to Ida B. Wells; recollections of childhood in the wilderness along the Mississippi and lines occasioned by urban incidents; invocations of the muse and addresses to an American beloved; reminiscences of a mulatress from Santo Domingo and poetological reflections in an age of censorship; somber elegies and whimsical poetic surprises; evocative songs about moonlight and rhymed animal fables with an attached moral.

It would be impossible to press these heterogeneous poems into the service of any single overarching interpretation. Yet they do fully convey the inwardness of a lost cultural moment, and whether these poems startle, amuse, or sadden the modern reader, they certainly do not generate indifference. In Norman Shapiro's excellent English translations and the facing French originals, they speak to readers in both languages. And they raise the question why the authors of these poems are not better known. Perhaps this collection will help to make the poets assembled here—Michel St. Pierre and Dominique Rouquette, M.-F. Liotau and Alfred Mercier, Victor Rillieux and Jules Choppin, Camille Thierry and Nicol Riquet, Adrien Rouquette, Tullius Saint-Céran, Charles-Oscar Dugué, and all the others—household words among modern readers in the United States, France, and elsewhere. *Creole Echoes* is a substantial contribution to the exploration of the multilingual legacy of the United States and of poetry in the French language.

Norman R. Shapiro

Preface

As we approach the bicentennial year of the Louisiana Purchase, it behooves us to remember that, for many decades, a large swath of land imposed a francophone presence alongside our burgeoning United States of America. Extending from North to South and fed by social and linguistic relations with "the French of France," by Canadian—Arcadian—immigration, and even by contact with a variety of the creolized French of the Caribbean, that presence became distilled, quintessentially, one might say, in and around the colorful and thriving port of New Orleans.

As a translator I find one of the joys of my craft in rediscovering texts that have long escaped notice and in re-creating them—reborn, as it were—for an English-language audience that probably never suspected their existence. (I say *re-creating* advisedly: for me, translation is, precisely, an exercise in re-creation, not a futile attempt at the exact duplication that some claim it, ideally, to be.) The translator often knows the thrill of discovery, even if in most cases it has to be, by definition, a rediscovery. But he or she knows the joy of creativity as well. Though always working with a text created by another, every translator, by choosing from a vast number of possibilities, leaves a personal mark on the work undertaken.

It is to Professor Lynn Weiss that I owe the first of these joys as afforded by the present collection. The French-language literary production of nineteenth-century New Orleans and surroundings was as unknown to me as, I suspect, it has been to most of my readers until she invited me, three years ago, to translate two plays by the francophone "free man of color" Victor Séjour. It was only after the publication of his powerful verse drama *Diégarias* (*The Jew of Seville*) and the no less compelling prose drama *La Tireuse de cartes* (*The Fortune-Teller*) that Professor Weiss convinced me to look as well into the wealth of poetry from that area, which had lain for almost a century and a half, only rarely disturbed by readers and scholars.

I will not pretend that I experienced an epiphany before a corpus of uniformly impressive literary quality. Nevertheless, I must be quick to admit that many of these almost unknown poets had produced a substantial canon that did not deserve the relative oblivion into which it had fallen. Here were works of a wide variety of inspirations and genres—classical, lyrical, historical, social, and even humorous (witness the rich body of fables in both French and Creole)—largely derivative and owing much to French models, to be sure, but often marked by a unique American flavor as well. Readers will find, I think, a certain quaint charm in French poems glorifying, along with the ever-present Mississippi (long since gallicized by Chateaubriand and others as the Méschacébé), historical figures like George Washington and Zachary Taylor and Civil War campaigns, all couched in patriotic encomium that reads curiously at odds with its French language and prosody. If it sounds much more appropriate in English translation, I hope the reader will not neglect to look from time to time at the French originals en face.

As ever, I have been guided in my translations—my re-creations—by the fundamental desire to carry across into English both the message of these poems and their manner. (Simplistic as this principle sounds, it bears repeating.) In so doing I have occasionally chosen to let some of the warts and blemishes show. To do otherwise would have been an act of infidelity. And no translator wants to be so carried away by the joys that the craft affords that the principle of faithfulness to the text gets lost in the enterprise.

M. Lynn Weiss

Introduction and Acknowledgments

The poetry collected in *Creole Echoes: The Francophone Poetry of Nineteenth-Century Louisiana* is part of a rich literary tradition that began in the late eighteenth century and continued well into the twentieth.[1] The tumultuous nineteenth century proved especially conducive to every aspect of literary activity, and in Louisiana francophone writing and publishing flourished. This bilingual volume of poetry is a small sample of the much greater archive that includes drama, short stories, and novels. The poets represented here reflect the three groups that created Louisiana's francophone literature: the Creoles, descendants of French or Spanish; Creoles of color, descendants of French or Spanish and Africans or Native Americans (known as "gens de couleur libres"); and "Frenchmen from France," the French émigrés who sought fortune or more often political asylum in Louisiana throughout the nineteenth century.[2]

These three groups and the writing they produced bear witness to a dynamic society that began the nineteenth century as a cast-off French possession and by century's end, saw the demise of a viable francophone community in the

United States. Directly or indirectly Louisiana was transformed by some of the most violent political and social revolutions of the nineteenth century. To summarize briefly, the United States purchased the colony from the French in 1803, and by 1810 refugees from the Haitian Revolution poured into New Orleans, increasing the population of Creoles of color. In the War of 1812 New Orleans was attacked by the British; during that same year Louisiana became a state, prompting an influx of anglophone settlers. In the 1840s large waves of immigrants from Ireland and Germany further destabilized the cultural and linguistic Creole community, and in 1830 and 1848 French refugees from the Louis-Philippe and Bonaparte III revolutions flocked to the United States, most coming to New Orleans. In 1862 New Orleans was defeated by the Union Army; two years later the first daily newspaper owned and operated by Creoles of color, *La Tribune de la Nouvelle Orléans,* was established to advocate civil rights. In 1866 a white mob attacked a mixed-race assembly convened to establish equal rights and universal male suffrage; dozens were killed in the Mechanics Hall massacre. In 1876 Creoles established a literary society to preserve French language and literature, but by 1896 only six French-language newspapers and journals were still in circulation. In 1914 the death knell sounded for the French language in Louisiana when the government ceased to require that its documents be published in French.[3] Against this volatile background, these Louisiana writers created an indigenous American literature in French.

The territory of Louisiana became a colony in 1699 and remained so until 1766, when the French crown gave it to Spain. Ironically French literature in Louisiana began in 1779, when Louisiana was no longer a French colony, with the publication of Julien Poydras's epic poem "La Prise du morne du Baton Rouge par Monseigneur Galvez." But arguably the most fecund period of literary production in francophone Louisiana began in the 1830s, and much of that literature appeared in newspapers and journals. Unlike the popular anthologies of nineteenth-century anglophone American poetry, only one anthology of francophone Louisiana literature was published in the nineteenth century.[4] In 1845 seventeen Creoles of color contributed eighty-two poems to a volume entitled *Les Cenelles: choix de poésies indigènes.*[5] Edited by the inimitable Creole of color Armand Lanusse, *Les Cenelles* underscores its indigenousness in the choice of symbol (cenelles are berries from the native hawthorn bush) and in its subtitle, *choix de poésies indigènes.* It was a highly self-conscious gesture by poets who did not want their work to "pass" into anthologies of French literature. Other avenues for publication lay open for the Creoles and French émigrés.

Louisiana's francophone writers typically submitted their work to one of New Orleans's newspapers or magazines that published poetry. Emigrés frequently started their own newspapers and became their own publishers, as did Charles Testut and Joseph Déjacque. In addition, an author with adequate funds might have a printer put together a collection of his or her work. Of the poets represented here, Emilie Evershed had two volumes of poetry published in Paris; the prolific Rouquette brothers had their volumes published in Paris and New Orleans; Alexandre Latil, Charles Testut, and Louis Allard had poetry collected and printed in New Orleans; and Camille Thierry's volume *Les Vagabondes* was published in Paris and Bordeaux. But most of the francophone literature produced in Louisiana first appeared in newspapers and literary journals. *L'Album littéraire: journal des jeunes gens, amateurs de littérature* (1843) featured the writing of the Creoles of color; the postbellum period gave birth to an African-American press that included *L'Union* (1863–64) and *La Tribune de la Nouvelle Orléans* (1864–69).[6] Poetry appeared in a number of Louisiana's newspapers, including *L'Abeille* (1827–1925), the *Revue louisianaise* (1846–48), and *Renaissance louisianaise* (1861–71). And the most important source for the postbellum literature is *Comptes-rendus de l'Athénée louisianais,* the literary journal of the association l'Athénée louisianais, which Alfred Mercier founded in 1876 to preserve the French language and literature in Louisiana.[7] A brief review of the history of francophone newspapers, magazines, and journals in Louisiana reveals the extent to which the print media were a vital source for native francophone literature. Moreover, this history can teach us much about the social and political relationships between the three segments of the francophone community: Creoles, Creoles of color, and French émigrés.

Louisiana's first francophone newspaper, *Le Moniteur de la Louisiane,* appeared in 1794, and it would remain the only such paper until 1803.[8] Although Louisiana's change in status from U.S. territory to state prompted the establishment of several more newspapers, it was not until 1830 that the newspapers began to print poetry, which they did only occasionally. In the next decade New Orleans emerged as one of the four most important ports in the United States, and the booming economy helped the number and variety of papers blossom. The early 1840s brought with them the first small weekly or monthly arts journals, of which *Revue louisianaise* (1846–48) was among the best.[9] Over half of the francophone newspapers and journals that "sprang up in Louisiana like mushrooms and died like flies" were begun by the so-called Frenchmen from France.[10] Refugees from the political revolutions in Haiti and France, these men came to New Orleans in three waves. The first group came from Haiti at the turn of the nineteenth century; the second group, exiles from the Louis-Philippe revolution, arrived in the 1830s; and the third wave were French Republicans proscribed by Napoléon III, who came between 1848 and 1851. At least half the writers and reporters for these newspapers numbered among this émigré population. The lack of profits in running a newspaper was no deterrent; in one instance the owner of a failed newspaper placed a sign in his shop window that read, "On the still smoking ruins, *L'Opinion* is resuscitated."[11] Throughout the nineteenth century, the social, political, and artistic lives of those in Louisiana's literate population were played out in the pages of the newspapers.

The antebellum period yielded no newspapers run by or catering to Creoles of color,[12] in part because of antiabolitionist laws that regulated publishing in Louisiana.[13] Fearful whites believed that Creoles of color would be tempted to challenge slavery and the violations of their own civil rights. In 1843 Armand Lanusse, an educator, a writer, and the editor of *Les Cenelles,* began *L'Album littéraire,* a literary journal that published works by Creoles and Creoles of color. *L'Album* was published bimonthly, probably edited by the Frenchman J. L. Marciacq, and had a short life; only four of the possibly six issues of *L'Album littéraire* survive.[14] Most of the work in the journal was unsigned or signed with initials only. According to Michel Fabre's reading of the extant copies, much of the writing is politically tame, although three of its pieces condemn *plaçage,* the practice whereby a young and usually fair-skinned Creole woman of color would be "placed"—that is, become the concubine of a wealthy white man—in exchange for a large sum of money, property, and future support. Such contracts were usually carried out by the *placée's* mother.[15] M.-F. Liotau's poem "Une Nouvelle Impression," an unsigned short story entitled "Marie," and Armand Lanusse's "Un Mariage de conscience" all depict the practice as a violation on multiple levels: *plaçage* violates the bond between mother and daughter, between the young woman and God, and between the man and his white wife.[16] Armand Lanusse's poem "Epigram," which appeared in *Les Cenelles* two years later (and is included in this volume), treats this theme as well.

The Creoles of color may not have had their own newspapers, but their poetry did appear in some of the city's publications. In the antebellum period, as Michel Fabre has observed, when there was no threat to the racial status quo, there was more cooperation than rivalry between the Creoles and their darker brothers. For example, in a June 1843 issue, *Le Courrier de la Louisiane* announced the publication of *L'Album littéraire.* The *Courrier* also published short stories by the Creole of color Michel Séligny, founder of the Sainte-Barbe Academy for the wealthy children of this community and the half-brother of poet Camille Thierry. The *Courrier* also published Séligny's 1856 review of the Creole of color Victor Séjour's play *Le Fils de la nuit,* then in production in Paris.[17] *La Renaissance louisianaise* published three of Séligny's short stories, and many of the poems Thierry published in *Les Vagabondes* (1874) had appeared in issues of *L'Orléanais* in the 1850s.[18] (Among

these "Fallen Woman," "Moonlight," and "To My American Miss" are includ-
ed in this volume.) Two Creoles of color crossed verbal swords in the pages
of *La Réforme* in April 1846. Liotau fired the initial salvo in this skirmish in
1845 when his poem "For a Friend Who Accused Me of Plagiarism" (includ-
ed here) appeared in *Les Cenelles*. Although their barbed verses were only ini-
tialed, Mirtil-Ferdinand Liotau attacked his opponent with satirical acrostics
that spelled Léon Sindos's full name.[19]

One of the most dramatic changes in Louisiana's print media occurred
during the Civil War immediately after New Orleans fell. In 1862 several mem-
bers of the Creole of color community launched *L'Union;* for the first time
Louisiana's Creoles of color openly criticized race-based violations of their civil
rights. Characterized as erudite and well written, *L'Union* was a "caste news-
paper" that assumed the distinction between the Creoles of color and the newly
freed bondsmen.[20] The paper's advocacy of civil rights for the Creoles of col-
or, especially the right to vote, so antagonized the white community of New
Orleans that repeated death threats stopped its publication in June 1864. Un-
daunted, the Creoles of color Dr. Louis-Charles and his brother Jean Rouda-
nez purchased the equipment and started publication of *La Tribune de la
Nouvelle Orléans* a month later. Unlike its predecessor, *La Tribune* purported
to be "the organ of the oppressed classes"; it would also be the first African
American daily paper. Roudanez persuaded Jean-Charles Houzeau, a distin-
guished Belgian astronomer and committed socialist, to become the paper's
editor. Houzeau, who had been exiled for his radical politics, was superbly
capable, diligent, and courageous in this position; he narrowly escaped mob
violence in the famous Mechanics Hall race riot of 1866 and returned to his
office to write a detailed account of the event. Under his direction *La Tribune*
became one of the most impressive papers the city ever had.[21] In addition to
running items from correspondents in Paris, Boston, and Mexico City, polit-
ical commentary from Armand Lanusse, and letters to the editor from lumi-
naries such as Garibaldi and Victor Hugo, *La Tribune* published the kind of
social protest poetry that had been prohibited before the war. *La Tribune*
published "The South's Constant Revolt," by "Henry" (probably the Creole
of color Henry Rey, an aspiring poet and spiritualist), on September 24, 1865,
and "To Père Chocarne," by "Pierre l'Hermite" (whose identity remains a
mystery), on June 16, 1867; both poems appear in the present volume.[22]

In the postbellum period the Frenchman Dr. Charles Testut founded
L'Equité in 1871. The short-lived paper, devoted to "universal progress," ex-
plicitly advocated the rights of the free people of color and the newly freed
bondsmen and -women. It also promoted freemasonry and attacked Catholi-
cism. Not surprisingly *L'Equité* folded after three issues. Despite the develop-
ment of a "black" press, Creoles of color continued to publish in "white" pa-

pers. Even though he used the pseudonym "Lélia D——t," Pierre Adolphe Duhart (included in this volume) first published poems in *Renaissance louisianaise* in 1862.[23] Two previously published poems by Camille Thierry were reprinted posthumously in *Comptes-rendus de l'Athénée louisianais* in January 1878. *Comptes-rendus* had already published "La Folle," by Lucien Mansion, in April 1886.[24] *Le Sud* and *The Crusader* were postwar newspapers that espoused the cause of all people of color, while *Le Carillon* launched a virulent campaign against Reconstruction, Yankees, Creoles of color, and the newly freed bondsmen.

Of all the publications begun in the postbellum period, *Comptes-rendus,* the organ for the Athénée louisianais, was wholly devoted to encouraging and supporting the production of French literature in Louisiana. The Athénée louisianais was a literary society founded in 1876 by several of New Orleans' elite Creoles, chief among them Dr. Alfred Mercier.[25] In his 1894 volume *Louisiana Studies* the historian Alcée Fortier wrote, "Our contemporary literature is contained almost exclusively in *Comptes-rendus de l'Athénée Louisianais.*"[26] Of the writers included in this volume, Stephen Bernard, Jules Choppin, Charles Deléry, Georges Dessommes, Edgar Grima, Joseph-Auguste-André Maltrait, Alfred Mercier, Léona Queyrouze, Dominique Rouquette, and Camille Thierry all saw their works appear in *Comptes-rendus,* which was published from 1876 to 1951. Despite this rich archive, some of the early histories of Louisiana's literature failed to consider the works published in newspapers and journals, even though the earliest study of francophone literature of Louisiana was published in *Le Courrier de la Louisiane* in 1847.[27] Louisiana's francophone newspapers and journals did not create an "imagined" community; rather, by publishing local writers, the print media facilitated the creation of an indigenous literature.

Most studies of Louisiana's francophone literature are greatly indebted to the work of Alcée Fortier. The descendant of an old Creole family, Fortier was a professor of French at Tulane University and the first president of the Modern Language Association. He was a prolific writer who sought to preserve and promote the francophone history and literature of Louisiana. He devoted his life to this end, completing numerous articles, essays, and books in both French and English before his death in 1914. Fortier's bibliography includes the groundbreaking 1886 essay "French Literature in Louisiana," the first scholarly survey of this literature.[28] Eight years later followed the first comprehensive history of Louisiana francophone literature: *Louisiana Studies: Literature, Customs and Dialects, History and Education,* published in 1894. Yet as Frans Amelinckx has observed, Fortier's work neglects literature that appeared in newspapers and magazines. Since much of the work of the French political exiles and the Creoles of color appeared in this forum, Fortier excluded these substantial contributions to the literature. In *Louisiana Studies* Fortier's focus comes to rest primarily on the writers defined as *"grands Creoles."* Most of these men were descendants of the original French and Spanish colonists and before the war constituted the economic, social, and cultural elite. *Louisiana Studies* also includes the work of some French émigrés and Creoles of color, although their race is never mentioned.[29] Fortier's study had an important impact on the way Louisiana's literary history would be written during the following fifty years.

In response to Fortier's silence on the subject, the Creole of color Rodolphe Desdunes published *Nos hommes et notre histoire* in 1911.[30] Notwithstanding some factual inaccuracies and its hagiographic impulses, the book remains a key source for the history of the Creoles of color, particularly the contributors to *Les Cenelles*. Alcée Fortier's son Edouard followed his father's lead in *Les Lettres françaises en Louisiane* (1915) by failing to identify the Creoles of color as such. More significant, a version of this essay became part of *The Cambridge History of American Literature* in the 1921, 1943, and 1965 editions.[31] Ruby Van Allen Caulfeild's 1929 survey of Louisiana's francophone literature, *The French Literature of Louisiana,* is admirably comprehensive. It includes poetry, drama, novels, and short stories, works that were published independently or in newspapers and journals. Caulfeild also includes a discussion of the large body of nonfiction writing, such as essays on yellow fever or lively critiques of George Washington Cable. Although she duly notes when an author is a native of Louisiana or a French émigré, Caulfeild neglects to identify the editor of and contributors to *Les Cenelles* as Creoles of color. Edward Larocque Tinker's monumental tome *Les Ecrits de langue française en Louisiane au XIX siècle* (1932) combines biography, bibliography, and literary criticism. Although subsequent studies have identified several factual errors and omissions in the volume, it was the first work to identify almost every published writer in the history of Louisiana, including racial identifications and bibliographies.[32] In 1937 Charles Roussève's book *The Negro in Louisiana* expanded the work begun in Desdunes's *Our People and Our History*. Auguste Viatte's *Histoire littéraire de l'Amérique française des origines à 1950* (1954) places Louisiana's literature in the larger context of New World francophone literature. But the mere eighty pages of the five-hundred-plus-page text devoted to Louisiana's literature made a new approach or novel observations impossible. Much to his credit, however, Viatte does acknowledge that the contributors to *Les Cenelles* were Creoles of color.[33] Virtually all these studies tend to read this francophone American literature through the lens of works by the great French romantic writers, such as Alexandre Dumas père, Victor Hugo, Alphonse de Lamartine, or Pierre-Jean de Béranger. Although these works were widely read and admired in Louisiana, and many Lousianans took inspiration from them, such an orientation can render only a partial understanding of Louisiana's francophone literature.

In *Revolution, Romanticism, and the Afro-Creole Protest Tradition in Louisiana, 1718–1868,* Caryn Cossé Bell makes the salient point that for some Creoles, most French émigrés, and all Creoles of color, what was particularly attractive in the work of Hugo, Lamartine, and Béranger was the successful combination of poetry and politics. True *artistes engagés,* this generation of romantic writers believed that the completion of the French Revolution depended on their depictions of social injustice and human misery. In 1818 Victor Hugo published *Bug-Jargal,* a novel set during the Haitian Revolution whose sympathetic hero is the leader of the resistance and an African king. Alphonse de Lamartine, arguably the greatest of the French romantic poets, wrote the drama *Toussaint Louverture* between 1839 and 1842, basing it on the leader of the Haitian Revolution. Lamartine was an advocate of universal suffrage and an active member of the Société française pour l'abolition de l'esclavage.[34] The poet and songwriter Pierre-Jean de Béranger was very popular among New Orleans's Creoles and Creoles of color. A man of great faith in the republican cause, Béranger placed his sympathies with the laboring classes, and he was a strong advocate of social reform.[35] References to Béranger and his work are everywhere; three of the *Les Cenelles* poets pay homage to him in their work. In this volume Alexandre Latil's "For Mademoiselle Adèle * * * " gives the great poet permission to change his verse, and Tullius Saint-Céran honors him in the couplet "Béranger."

The beliefs animating the poetry of these French romantic writers included an abiding faith in the ideals of the French Revolution and the notion that a society built on liberty, equality, and brotherhood is not only possible but imperative. This had special resonance for the Creoles of color who lived in a republic that accorded them few civil rights. For French émigrés such as the radical socialist Joseph Déjacque, whose volume *Les Lazaréennes* was ordered destroyed by the French government, Louisiana embodied the failure of these revolutionary principles. Déjacque's work asks whether a democratic republic is possible in the context of capitalism and slavery. Charles Testut's writing was less hostile but no less radical than Déjacque's. Testut's abolitionist novel *Le Vieux Solomon,* completed in 1858 but not published until 1872, as well as his public advocacy of civil rights for freemen and Creoles of color, won him the unmitigated antipathy of his Creole audience. At long last, the Civil War made it possible for Creoles of color to openly and explicitly criticize the racist social and political order of Louisiana. To Armand Lanusse's bitterly ironic antebellum "Epigram" were added Pierre l'Hermite's "To Père Chocarne" and Victor Rillieux's "Love and Devotion," in which Ida B. Wells, the brave black journalist whose antilynching campaign endangered her own life, is compared to Judith and Joan of Arc. "The South's Constant Revolt" decried the postbellum efforts to reestablish the antebellum racial order. Louisiana's poets adopted the poetics and often the politics of Hugo, Lamartine, or Béranger for the American context. After France's 1848 revolution failed, Dominique Rouquette proudly boasted of American democracy and specifically of the election of the Louisianan Zachary Taylor as president of the United States in "For Monsieur Hilarion Huc":

> Ah, yes! America chooses the best,
> Most noble: fine example for you, France!
> The Presidency is the worthiest
> Honor that talent and proud circumstance
> Bestow!... Poor France!—Ship mastless, rudderless—
> Alas! Alack! You waver to and fro,
> Victim of your aimless capriciousness!

Similarly, in the poem "A Monsieur de Chateaubriand," Adrien Rouquette praises the great poet but then takes issue with Chateaubriand's *Atala,* a novella with a Native American heroine who symbolizes the New World. Failing to recognize Louisiana or the Choctaw in Chateaubriand's rendering, Rouquette then asks: "Tell me poet, did you see my native land before you described it?"[36] The question implicitly disqualifies Chateaubriand from writing authentic Louisiana poetry. Rouquette placed this poem at the beginning of his collection *Les Savanes: poésies américaines,* and the remaining poems take up the task of rendering an authentic portrait of his native land. As the title suggests, these are American poems from the pen of a proud Creole; other poems in the collection include "The Young Choctaw," "To My Native Town," "Regrets of a Young Creole Student Exiled in Paris," "Recollection of Kentucky," and "Evening Stroll on the Levee" (the last two included here). Just as romanticism inspired anglophone American poets to find in nature the truest expression of God and one's authentic self, the francophone poets looked to Louisiana's bayous, its flora and fauna, the Mississippi, and the Choctaw as sources for their poetry and identity. Charles-Oscar Dugué's "Memories of the Wilderness" links God with nature and poetry:

> O fair Louisiana! O you vast
> Cypress groves where, alone, in days long past,
> My footsteps strayed—a dreamer then, although
> But a mere lad!—and where I used to go,
> As in some holy place, a-wandering, awed,
> To listen to the mighty voice of God;
> Where I would hear vague harmonies, and let
> Myself converse, in sacred *tête-à-tête,*

With gentle Spirits! O my New World sky,
Where poetry once rained with tearful cry.

Adrien Rouquette's "Recollection of Kentucky" employs a similar conceit.

Mere child, I wandered through Kentucky's wild,
Unconquered nature... Ah! When, but a child,
One sees the forest's beauty, never can
The memory fade when he grows to a man!

In "Fatherland" Alfred Mercier employs the gallicized word for Mississippi in the description of his homecoming:

O Meschacebé! You saw me rejoice
In childish games by your resounding shore;
Father of Waters, you see me once more
Leap, drunk with joy, to hear your long-drawn voice!

Here the great river, the "father of waters," reinforces the father in "Fatherland."

Another important thread in the fabric of romantic thought was the idea that the cultural productions of the folk express the genius of a people. In the francophone poetry of Louisiana the authentic voice often spoke in black dialect. Several poets assumed this voice to narrate fables with figures inspired by African animal tricksters as well as those of La Fontaine. "Pa Guitin" narrates Jules Choppin's poem "The Hare and the Tortoise," and "The Oak and the Reed" contains this message for the high and mighty: "Don't go make boast, one day you go lay flat: / Big papa lion, him scared of little rat." Edgar Grima adopted a similar voice in "The Wolf and the Stork." Although not told in dialect, Joseph Maltrait's "The Melon" critiques Creole greed and cruelty to slaves with an ending that still shocks. Camille Thierry's "An Old Mulatress's Lament" is another brilliant illustration of the black Creole dialect that speaks to the "miscegenated" origins of the francophone "new" world.

Les Cenelles was dedicated to Louisiana's fairer sex, and the following pages include several poems that may have been written at the request of a young belle or, as Michel Fabre has suggested, as entertainment.[37] One such example is Pierre Dalcour's "Lines Written in the Album of Mademoiselle * * * ":

The star that twinkles high in heaven's expanse,
The moonlight, gentle, in the darkening skies,
Are not so sweet to look on as a glance
From your brown-lidded eyes.

Other odes to beauty are predictable: Louis Allard's "Niagara" equates this natural wonder to the beauty of his own true love. Oscar Dugué's "Memory of the Ball" and "Love" embellish these simpler conceits, and in a slight variation, Mirtil-Ferdinand Liotau's "For Ida" declares that a young belle's beauty is less striking than her virtue. In Camille Thierry's playful "Moonlight" the lover implores the moon to conceal its beauty so that the beauty whose arrival he awaits will be willing to reveal her own. Among the familiar themes of lost love (Dugué's "Jealousy"), forbidden love (Latil's "For Corinne * * * "), and frustrated love (Rillieux's "The Coward"), there is also beauty that devastates, as in Louis Allard's "On the Portrait of * * *." The more sinister faces of love appear in Camille Thierry's "To My American Miss," who may well be a willisprite, the angry spirit of a spurned lover, and in Thierry's eerie Baudelairian poem "The Incubus," wherein a beauty is destroyed by a vengeful spirit. Francophone love poems are frequently sexual in nature, an aspect less familiar in romantic anglophone poetry. In Louis-Armand Garreau's "For Nina" a lovesick youth declares his passion for a very expensive prostitute; similarly, Thierry's poem "The Fallen Woman" recalls its subject's innocence with little regret. Again, Thierry's "An Old Mulatress's Lament" is explicit about the nature of its speaker's relationship to white men:

> Listen! Way back, Santo Domingo,
> Black girls, them be like jewels! Just so!
> White men, them pester us, them cling, oh!
> Follow us everywhere we go.
>> Them live with us,
>> No fight, no fuss.
> Love us like goddesses, worship, embrace!
>> Them never cheap,
>> Them pockets, deep:
> Give what men want, them give us run of place!

Among these great beauties are the Creole women of color: Liotau's "Ida" with her dark eyes and ebony tresses, "the brown-lidded" beauty of Dalcour's "Lines," and the daughter in Lanusse's "Epigram" are all women of color.

French romanticism certainly exerted an important influence on Louisiana's writers, but the romantic poetry of francophone Louisiana nevertheless described and illuminated a vibrant linguistic community that, aware of its own fragile existence, took every occasion to express its originality.

Frans Amelinckx has noted that the largest obstacle to an appreciation of francophone contributions to American literature is the inaccessibility of the texts in either French or English translation. *The Louisiana Book: Selections from the Literature of the State,* published in 1894, was one of the first anthologies of this material. Its editor, Thomas M'Caleb, made the following point in his preface: "The singular fact that the literature of Louisiana speaks both in the French and English tongue has generally been unnoticed by historians of American letters."[38] M'Caleb further explained that the market dictated that he exclude any French material, adding that most francophone Louisianans were fluent in English—and thereby missing the point completely. The editors of the seventeen-volume *Library of Southern Literature* (1907–9) did include excerpts from works by the dramatist Placide Canonge, poetry by Adrien and Dominique Rouquette, and two poems by Alfred Mercier, as well as an excerpt from his novel *L'Habitation Saint-Ybars*.[39] Although this offering is minuscule in a multivolume work, it is one of the rare instances in which non-anglophone American literature appears, untranslated, in an anthology of southern literature. Looking at the numerous anthologies of African American literature published in the twentieth century, I found only two that included poems from *Les Cenelles*.[40] Apart from these instances, collections of Louisiana's literature remained as segregated as the Jim Crow South.

Twentieth-century anthologies of Louisiana's francophone literature include Edward Maceo Coleman's *Creole Voices: Poems in French by Free Men of Color: First Published in 1845*.[41] This centennial edition also included poems by Victor Rillieux and Rodolphe Desdunes. Auguste Viatte published *Anthologie littéraire de l'Amérique francophone* in 1971. This volume is a companion piece to his 1954 study *Histoire littéraire de l'Amérique française* and devotes only fifty-five pages to Louisiana's literature.[42] In 1979 a bilingual edition of *Les Cenelles* was published; Régine Latortue and Gleason Adams's translation is entitled *Les Cenelles: A Collection of Poems by Creole Writers of the Early 19th Century*. That same year Gérard St. Martin and Jacqueline Voorhies edited the anthology *Écrits louisianais du dix-neuvime siècle: nouvelles, contes et fables*.[43] In 1981 Barry Ancelet and Mathé Allain published *Littérature française de la Louisiane*. This volume includes work from the eighteenth, nineteenth, and twentieth centuries, but the emphasis is on the twentieth. And more recently James Cowan edited *La Marseillaise noire et autres poèmes de la Nouvelle Orléans* in 2001.[44] Langston Hughes translated two poems from *Les Cenelles*, Armand Lanusse's "Epigram" and Dalcour's "Lines Written in the Album of Mademoiselle * * *," and included them in *The Langston Hughes Reader*.[45] In the past ten years a number of texts from francophone Louisiana's archive have been published in French and in translation.[46] The facts and features of this archive compel literary historians to reconsider long-held assumptions about our national literature.

The francophone writing by Louisiana's Creoles of color has dramatically altered our literary history's time line. For example, it was long believed that Ellen Frances Watkins Harper's story "The Two Offers" (1859) was the first by an African American. In fact, Louisiana's Victor Séjour was the first American of African descent to publish a short story; "The Mulatto" appeared in 1837.[47] Séjour also has the honor of being the first American man of color to publish a play, *Diégarias* (*The Jew of Seville*) in 1844; this play was performed by the Comédie-Française in the same year. And as we have seen, *Les Cenelles: choix de poésies indigènes* is the first anthology of African American and francophone American literature. The francophone writings challenge current characterizations of nineteenth-century American literature based solely on anglophone writing. As noted previously, francophone Louisiana's romantic poetry is more frank about the sexual nature of romantic love and consequently makes explicit topics rare in anglophone literature, such as prostitution and concubinage. Alfred Mercier's 1877 novel *The Priest's Daughter* is a critique of celibacy in the Catholic church, and his 1891 novel *Johnelle* deals with abortion. Victor Séjour's characterization of slavery and the "mulatto" is the polar opposite of William Wells Brown's Clotel in *Clotel: Or the President's Daughter* or Dion Boucicault's Zoe in *The Octoroon*. Always implied or muted in anglophone writings, the white master's sexual assault on his female slaves is explicit in Séjour's story "The Mulatto." To underscore their status as victims, most anglophone mulatto characters were female. But Victor Séjour's mulatto Georges manages a terrible revenge on his white master/father, killing him, his wife, and newborn child before killing himself. As Werner Sollors has observed, the violent oedipal conflict in this story anticipates themes of twentieth-century African American literature as seen in works such as Claude McKay's poem "Mulatto" and Langston Hughes's story "Father and Son" and play *Mulatto*.[48] The Creole Sidonie de la Houssaye's serialized novel *The Quadroons of New Orleans* offers yet another rendering of this character.

Equally important are the ways in which this francophone literature expands and complicates our understanding of the nineteenth-century writers' engagement with the politics and poetics of France and the Caribbean. For example, the Paris-based abolitionist journal in which Séjour's story was published, *Revue des colonies,* had been founded by Cyrille Bissette, a Creole of color from Martinique. In addition, "The Mulatto" is set on the island of Saint-Domingue, or as the narrator reminds us, "today the republic of Haiti." And many collections of Louisiana francophone poetry were first published in Paris, while New Orleans's newspapers and journals published all the latest work of Hugo, Lamartine, and Béranger. In this context, the francophone poets, many educated in Paris, negotiated a complex identity that anticipated many features of the contemporary transnational, bicultural, and certainly bilingual postmodern identity.

The francophone poetry, fiction, and drama of Louisiana contribute to a more complex understanding of the multilingual origins of American literature and culture. In our public debates, the multilingual dimension of America's multicultural origins receives little attention. The focus tends to remain on categories of racial or ethnic difference. And as Werner Sollors has observed, "the absence of language as a variable in the debate may have contributed to the dominance of racially based identifications and the pervasiveness of identity politics."[49] In view of Louisiana's francophone community, is it possible to talk about cultural diversity without discussing language? Long before waves of European immigrants transformed Manhattan's Lower East Side into Babel after-the-fall, Louisiana was arguably the most multicultural of places in North America. Spanish, French, several Native American and African tribes, refugees from Haiti, and the offspring of intergroup unions made up the territory's population. Louisiana's francophone literature reminds us that during the eighteenth and nineteenth centuries, French was not a foreign language in Louisiana. It is our hope that *Creole Echoes: The Francophone Literature of Nineteenth-Century Louisiana* will contribute to a greater understanding of and appreciation for Louisiana's considerable gifts to American literature.

A Note on Sources

The material for this collection came from several sources. Most of the poems were taken from volumes originally published in the nineteenth century. These texts often contained printer's errors in spelling, punctuation, and diacritical notation. Where these errors were obvious, we corrected them. Some of the poems appeared only in the journal *Comptes-rendus*. The poems that appeared in the *New Orleans Tribune* were taken from the Marcus B. Christian Collection in the Archives and Manuscripts Department of the Earl K. Long Library of the University of New Orleans. In Paris, Michel Fabre supported this research by generously sharing his extensive archival material. For biographical information on the poets, I relied on the substantial body of work cited in the introduction to this volume.

Acknowledgments

My sincere thanks to the scholars Caryn Cossé Bell, George Aaron Broadwell, Rick Griffiths, Dana Kress, Jack B. Martin, and David C. Rankin for expert and timely instruction. Many thanks, too, to Janet Elsasser and Cynthia Mack, librarians at the College of William and Mary; a faculty research grant from the College of William and Mary helped me to complete the manuscript. I am grateful to the Fulbright Program for the fellowship that enabled me to conduct some of the research for this project at the Bibliothèque Nationale in Paris; *merci mille fois* to the Franco-American Commission for Educational Exchange and to Valérie Géraud and Michèle Valencia for their kindness and support *sur place*. I am ever grateful to Werner Sollors for his encouragement and guidance. Many thanks are due Willis Regier for his ongoing commitment to the recuperation of lost treasures. It has been a great pleasure to work with Norman Shapiro on this project, and I am most grateful to him for his kindness, good humor, generosity, and dedication.

My greatest debt is to Michel Fabre, whose work made this and so many other projects possible, and to whom this volume is gratefully dedicated.

Notes

1. Frans Amelinckx, "La Littérature louisianaise au xix siècle," *Présence francophone* 43 (1993): 11. My introductory essay is greatly indebted to Frans Amelinckx's instructive and insightful article.

2. Throughout the text, I use the terms *Creole* to refer to descendants of French and Spanish settlers of Louisiana and *Creole of color* to refer to men and women whose ancestry included French or Spanish and African or Native Americans who were born free in the so-called New World. During the eighteenth and nineteenth centuries, Creoles of color were referred to as "gens de couleur libres," or "free people of color." By omitting the term *Creole,* this appellation distances these people from their French and Spanish origins. In *Our People and Our History* Rodolphe Desdunes uses the term *Creole of color* to insist on his community's relationship to the Creoles and to the history of Louisiana. The Acadians were a significant part of Louisiana's francophone community, which also included émigrés from Belgium and the French Caribbean.

3. Amelinckx, "La Littérature louisianaise," 15–17; Auguste Viatte, *Histoire littéraire de l'Amérique française des origines à 1950* (Paris: Presses Universitaires de France, 1954), 298–99; Caroline Senter, "Creole Poets on the Verge of a Nation," in *Creole: The History and Legacy of Louisiana's Free People of Color,* ed. Sybil Kein (Baton Rouge: Louisiana State University Press, 2000), 276–78.

4. For example, four separate volumes of poetry by American women appeared between 1842 and 1850: Rufus Wilmot Griswold, ed., *Gems from the American Female Poets* (1842); Caroline May, ed., *Female Poets of America* (1848); Rufus Wilmot Griswold, ed., *The Female Poets of America* (1849); and Thomas Read, ed., *The Female Poets of America* (1850).

5. Armand Lanusse, ed., *Les Cenelles: choix de poésies indigènes* (1845).

6. Michel Fabre, "The New Orleans Press and French-Language Literature by Creoles of Color," in *Multilingual America: Transnationalism, Ethnicity, and the Languages of American Literature,* ed. Werner Sollors (New York: New York University Press, 1998), 29–30.

7. Edward Larocque Tinker, *Les Ecrits de langue française en Louisiane au 19ème siècle* (Paris: Librairie Ancienne Honoré Champion, 1932), 356.

8. Edward Larocque Tinker, *Bibliography of the French Newspapers and Periodicals of Louisiana* (Worcester, Mass.: American Antiquarian Society, 1933), 12.

9. Tinker, *Bibliography,* 13–14.

10. Ibid., 5, 12.

11. Ibid., 13.

12. Fabre, "New Orleans Press," 29.

13. Caryn Cossé Bell, *Revolution, Romanticism, and the Afro-Creole Protest Tradition in Louisiana, 1718–1868* (Baton Rouge: Louisiana State University Press, 1997), 93–94.

14. Fabre, "New Orleans Press," 30, 48; Tinker, *Bibliography,* 39.

15. Joan Martin, "*Plaçage* and the Louisiana *Gens de Couleur Libres:* How Race and Sex Defined the Lifestyles of Free Women of Color," in *Creole: The History and Legacy of Louisi-*

ana's *Free People of Color,* ed. Sybil Kein (Baton Rouge: Louisiana State University Press, 2000), 57–70. In her dissertation in progress, "'They Call it Marriage': Interracial Families in Post-emancipation Louisiana," Diana Williams reports that the noun *plaçage* does not appear in any of the primary sources cited in secondary sources on this topic. Williams speculates that the term *plaçage* "crept into the literature via Frazier's relationship with Melville Herskovitz, who used it in reference to his work in Haiti" (personal correspondence, November 11, 2002; Williams is a student in the history of American civilization at Harvard University).

16. Fabre, "New Orleans Press," 31–32.

17. Ibid., 39.

18. Ibid.; Auguste Viatte, "Complément à la bibliographie louisianaise d'Edward Larocque Tinker," *Revue de Louisiane* 3, no. 2 (1974): 47.

19. Fabre, "New Orleans Press," 37.

20. Ibid., 40.

21. Jean-Charles Houzeau, *My Passage at the New Orleans Tribune: A Memoir of the Civil War Era,* intro. and ed. David Rankin, trans. Gerard Denault (Baton Rouge: Louisiana State University Press, 1984). This book is an English-language translation of a two-part article by Houzeau, "Le Journal noir aux Etats-Unis de 1863 à 1870," *Revue de Belgique* 11 (May 15, 1872): 5–28 and (June 15, 1872): 97–122.

22. Ibid., 41; Tinker, *Bibliography,* 21.

23. Viatte, "Complément," 27–28.

24. Charles Barthelemy Roussève, *The Negro in Louisiana: Aspects of His History and His Literature* (New Orleans: Xavier University Press, 1937), 115–16.

25. Ruby Van Allen Caulfeild, *The French Literature of Louisiana* (New York: Institute of French Studies, Columbia University Press, 1929), 64; Tinker, *Ecrits,* 356; Roussève, *Negro in Louisiana,* 114; Viatte, *Histoire,* 282. Caulfeild, Tinker, and Viatte indicate that l'Athénée was founded in 1876, but Roussève has given 1875 as the year. In *Louisiana Studies: Literature, Customs and Dialects, History and Education* (1894), Alcée Fortier gives no date for the founding of the society but notes that the first volume of *Comptes-rendus* was issued in 1876.

26. Fortier, *Louisiana Studies,* 64.

27. Amelinckx, "La Littérature louisianaise," 17.

28. Alcée Fortier, "French Literature in Louisiana," *PMLA* 2 (1886): 31–60.

29. Amelinckx, "La Littérature louisianaise," 17–18.

30. Rodolphe Desdunes, *Nos hommes et notre histoire* (Montréal: Arbour et Dupont, 1911); English-language trans., Desdunes, *Our People and Our History,* trans. and ed. Sister Dorothea Olga McCants (Baton Rouge: Louisiana State University Press, 1973).

31. Edouard Fortier, *Les Lettres françaises en Louisiane* (Québec: Imprimerie l'Action Sociale Limite, 1915), 3–25; William Trent, ed., *The Cambridge History of American Literature,* 4 vols. (New York: Putnam's, 1921); William Trent, ed., *The Cambridge History of American Literature,* 3 vols. (New York: Macmillan, 1943); William Trent, ed., *The Cambridge History of American Literature,* 3 vols. (New York: Macmillan, 1965).

32. Viatte, "Complément," 12–57.

33. Despite its efforts to contextualize Louisiana's literature within social and political milieux, Réginald Hamel's two-volume *La Louisiane Créole littéraire, politique et sociale, 1762–1900* (Ottawa: Les Editions Leméac, 1984) adds little to the existing studies.

34. Bell, *Revolution,* 98–99.

35. Ibid., 121.

36. Adrien Rouquette, *Les Savanes: poésies américaines* (1841).

37. Fabre, "New Orleans Press," 35.

38. Thomas M'Caleb, *Louisiana Book: Selections from the Literature of the State* (1894).

39. Edwin Anderson Alderman, ed., *Library of Southern Literature*, 17 vols. (Atlanta: Martin and Hoyt, 1909), vols. 2, 8, and 10. Volume 4 includes historical essays by Alcée Fortier and Charles Gayarré.

40. William Robinson, ed., *Early Black American Poets* (Dubuque, Iowa: Wm. C. Brown, 1968); Jerry Ward Jr., ed., *Trouble the Water: Two-Hundred Fifty Years of African American Poetry* (New York: Penguin, 1997).

41. Edward Maceo Coleman, ed., *Creole Voices: Poems in French by Free Men of Color: First Published in 1845* (Washington, D.C.: Associated, 1945).

42. Auguste Viatte, *Anthologie littéraire de l'Amérique francophone* (Québec: Sherbrooke University, 1971).

43. Gérard St. Martin and Jacqueline Voorhies, eds., *Ecrits louisianais du dix-neuvième siècle* (Baton Rouge: Louisiana State University Press, 1979).

44. Barry Ancelet and Mathé Allain, *Littérature française de la Louisiane* (Bedford, N.H.: National Materials Development Center for French, 1981); James Cowan, *La Marseillaise noire et autre poèmes de la Nouvelle Orléans* (Lyon: Editions du Cosmogone, 2001).

45. Langston Hughes, *The Langston Hughes Reader* (New York: George Braziller, 1958), 136.

46. Amelinckx,"La Littérature louisianaise," 20. There are important ongoing efforts to make this material available, and the Tintamarre on-line library at Louisiana's Centenary College is a particularly valuable source. In addition to offering the poetry of Louis Allard, Dominique Rouquette, and others, it includes the novel *l'Habitation Saint-Ybars*, by Alfred Mercier. Recent publications in French include Georges Dessommes's *Tante Cydette*, ed. Eve Heckenbach (Gretna, La.: Pelican, 2001); *La Marseillaise noire*, ed. Cowan; *Michel Séligny: homme de couleur de la Nouvelle Orléans, nouvelles et récits*, ed. Frans Amelinckx (Québec: Les Presses de l'Université Laval, 1998); Sidonie de la Houssaye's *Pouponne et Balthazar*, ed. May Waggoner (Lafayette: Center for Louisiana Studies, 1983); Alfred Mercier's *L'Habitation Saint-Ybars*, ed. Réginald Hamel (Bedford, N.H.: National Materials Development Center for French, 1982); *Littérature française de la Louisiane*, ed. Barry Ancelet and Mathé Allain (Bedford, N.H.: National Materials Development Center for French, 1981); and *Ecrits louisianais du dix-neuvième siècle*, ed. Gérard St. Martin and Jacqueline Voorhies (Baton Rouge: Louisiana State University Press, 1979). Texts now available in English translation include the following works by Victor Séjour: *The Brown Overcoat*, trans. Pat Hecht, in *Black Theatre USA: Plays by African Americans*, 2 vols., ed. James Hatch and Ted Shine (New York: Free Press, 1996), vol. 1; *The Jew of Seville*, trans. Norman Shapiro, ed. Lynn Weiss (Urbana: University of Illinois Press, 2002); *The Fortune-Teller*, trans. Norman Shapiro, ed. Lynn Weiss (Urbana: University of Illinois Press, 2002); "The Mulatto," trans. Andrea Lee, in *The Multilingual Anthology of American Literature*, ed. Marc Shell and Werner Sollors (New York: New York University Press, 2001); and *Les Cenelles: A Collection of Poems by Creole Writers of the Early Nineteenth Century*, trans. and ed. Régine Latortue and Gleason Adams (Boston: G. K. Hall, 1979).

47. Shell and Sollors, *Multilingual Anthology*, 714n2.

48. Werner Sollors, *Neither Black nor White yet Both: Thematic Explorations of Interracial Literature* (New York: Oxford University Press, 1997), 475n11.

49. Werner Sollors, ed., *Multilingual America: Transnationalism, Ethnicity, and the Languages of American Literature* (New York: New York University Press, 1998), 4.

Creole Echoes

Pour le Portrait de * * *

Ah! redoutez de voir l'objet
Que représente ce portrait.
O vous qui chérissez la vie:
Cette beauté fait sans retour
Mourir tous les hommes d'amour,
Et les femmes de jalousie.

Louis Allard (1777–1847)

Louis Allard was born in New Orleans to a wealthy Creole family in 1777. The Allard plantation made up most of what is today one of New Orleans's largest public parks. Educated in France, Allard became an accomplished Latinist. Allard had no interest in the world of business, and the estate his father left him slowly diminished as Allard sold it to support himself. Toward the end of his life the once-wealthy Louis Allard was virtually penniless and had to sell what remained of his land. The new proprietor permitted him to live on the property until his death in 1847; he was buried on his family's former estate. The property was later donated to the city of New Orleans.

Louis Allard's only collection of poetry, *Les Epaves,* was published in Paris and New Orleans in May 1847, within days of his death, with only "un Louisianais" appearing on the volume's title page. This stratagem supported the ruse suggested in the preface, which claimed the collection to be beached wreckage from the steamboat *Hecla.* Here the term *épaves* means "flotsam" or "refuse." Several poems in *Les Epaves* are renderings of the epigrams of the Roman poet Martial (the Latin originals, in italic, appear here following the French versions).

There is a complete on-line copy of *Les Epaves* at Centenary College's Tintamarre collection <http://www.centenary.edu/departme/french/epaves>.

On the Portrait of * * *

Who loves life can do nothing worse
Than look on her whom this, my verse,
Portrays: her face will deadly be,
Nor is there any cure thereof.
Men look and, straightway, die of love;
And women too, of jealousy.

Niagara

Cascade de Niagara,
Sous l'épais berceau de ton onde,
Je viens du nom de Louisa
Laisser l'impression profonde;
Mais si ma main gravait ses traits
Sur cette roche humide et brune,
Ici l'on pourrait désormais
Voir deux merveilles au lieu d'une.

Au Moqueur

Charmant oiseau, dont le savant ramage
Sait imiter par des accents divers,
De mille oiseaux qui peuplent le bocage,
Les doux accords et les brillants concerts.

Lorsque ta voix mélodieuse et pure
Vient enchanter les plaines et les bois;
Ou se mêler à l'onde qui murmure,
Je sens ravir tous mes sens à la fois.

Comme le mal qui circule en nos veines
Cède aux vertus d'un baume bienfaisant,
Ainsi, toujours mes chagrins et mes peines
Sont suspendus ou guéris par ton chant.

Pour imiter les airs que tu soupires,
L'art des mortels ferait de vains efforts;
Les séraphins pourraient seuls sur leurs lyres,
Rivaliser tes sublimes accords.

A * * *, en Voyant Son Portrait

En voyant tes divins attraits,
D'amour je ne puis me défendre;
Et pour Vénus je te prendrais
Si tu voulais te laisser prendre.

Niagara

Here, to your rushing falls, I came,
Niagara, and have carved behind
Your lulling roar Louisa's name
In letters deep... If one should find,
One day, that name thus left by me,
Graven in rock, wet, dark of hue,
He would behold, assuredly,
Not one mere marvel here, but two.

To the Mockingbird

Delightful bird, whose clever voice can sing
In many an accent, mimicking all those
Thousands of woodland songsters, echoing
Soft coos and virtuoso tremolos...

When your pure voice enchants the countryside's
Meadows and groves with its lush melody,
Or mingles with the hushed flow of the tides,
My senses, all at once, enrapture me.

Just as the virtue of a healing balm
Subdues the pain that plies our bodies, so
In like wise does your song forever calm,
And even cure, my soul's most grievous woe.

Man's art is powerless to make of him
Your equal, with his airs, however fine;
For, on their lyres, none but the seraphim
Rival, with theirs, your harmonies divine.

For * * *, on Seeing Her Portrait

Before your charms divine I fight
In vain: love leaves me bruised and shaken;
For Venus I should take you, might
You let yourself, alas, be taken.

L'Amour Enfant

Vous demandez, belle Thémire
Pourquoi l'on peint toujours l'amour comme un enfant?
Hélas! il faut bien vous le dire:
C'est que jamais l'amour n'est plus grand qu'en naissant!

A Priscus

Priscus, avant de te connaître,
Je t'appelais mon seigneur et mon maître;
Aussitôt que je te connus,
Je t'appelai Priscus, et rien de plus.

In Priscum

Quum te non nossem, dominum regemque vocabam:
Nunc bene te novi, iam mihi Priscum eris.

(Martial I.112)

A une Femme Belle et Difforme

Dieux! quels attraits divins ton voile nous dérobe!
Mais, las! quel corps affreux tu nous montres au bain!
Si tu veux obtenir un triomphe certain,
Relève bien ton voile, et baisse bien ta robe.

In mulierem deformem

Formosam faciem nigro velamine celas:
Sed non formoso corpore lædis aquas.
Ipsam crede deam verbis tibi dicere nostris:
"Aut aperi faciem, aut tunicata lava."

(Martial III.3)

Child Cupid

You ask, O fair Thémire, why, ever,
Love is a babe portrayed. Well, verily,
    The answer is, alas, that never
Will he grow bigger than at birth is he.

To Priscus

Priscus, back in the days before
We met, I called you "lord and master"; then
We met, and when I spoke of you again,
    I called you "Priscus," nothing more.

To a Beautiful and Misshapen Woman

Divine, the face your veil conceals! But oh!
We see your body in the bath... No! Frightful!...
Would you win hearts? Would you be thought delightful?
Lift high your veil, and let your gown hang low.

A Cinna

Quelque chose que tu me demandes,
Suivant toi, ce n'est rien. Eh bien!
Je ne te refuse donc rien,
Quand je refuse tes demandes!

In Cinnam

Esse nihil dicis quidquid petis, improbe Cinna:
Si nil, Cinna, petis, nil tibi, Cinna, nego.

(Martial III.61)

A Emile

Pauvre aujourd'hui, demain tu le seras encore:
C'est vers le riche seul que l'on voit couler l'or.

Ad Æmilianuum

Semper pauper eris, si pauper es, Æmiliane.
Dantur opes nulli nunc nisi divitibus.

(Martial V.81)

De Paulla

Ces cheveux sont à moi, dit Paulla, je le jure.
Qui pourrait l'appeler parjure?
Qui pourrait dire qu'elle ment?
Ils ont par elle été payés comptant.

De Fabulla

Iurat capillos esse, quos emit, suos
Fabulla: numquid, Paulle, peierat? nego.

(Martial VI.12)

For Cinna

Something you ask of me; but then
You say it's nothing, little more.
Well! I deny you nothing when
I deny what you ask me for!

For Emile

Pauper today, pauper tomorrow still:
Gold flows to none but those who have their fill!

On Paulla

"This hair," says Paulla, "is all mine, I swear!"
    Does she swear false? Is it her hair?
    Does she speak lies? Nay, not a whit!
Her hair? Of course it is!... She paid for it.

A Bithynicus

Quand Thélès ne voyait que des gens vertueux,
Il n'avait rien. Sa toge avait à peine l'âme;
Il a de tout: de l'or, des meubles somptueux,
    Depuis qu'il hante une jeunesse infâme.
Bithynicus, veux-tu devenir opulent?
       De l'impudicité, du vice,
      Comme lui deviens le complice;
De nos jours, la vertu ne donne pas d'argent.

De Thelesino

Quum coleret puros pauper Thelesinus amicos,
    Errabat gelida sordidus in togula:
Obscœnos ex quo cœpit curare cinœdos .
    Argentum, mensas, prædia solus emit.
Vis fieri dives, Bithynice? conscius esto.
    Nil tibi vel minimum basia pura dabunt.

   (Martial VI.50)

Les Bons Epoux

   Tous deux méchants, tous deux infâmes,
Toi le pire mari, toi la pire des femmes,
   Avec raison on est surpris
Que vous ne viviez pas comme de bons amis.

In Pessimos Conjuges

Quum sitis similes paresque vita,
Uxor pessima, pessimus maritus,
Miror non bene convenire vobis.

   (Martial VIII.35)

To Bithynicus

When Theles with but virtuous men consorted,
Naught did he own: threadbare, his toga was
A ghost! Today, great wealth is his. The cause?
He has, alas, with shameless youth cavorted.
Would you, like him, grow rich, Bithynicus?
 Then do as he; throw in your lot
 With vice, misspent and misbegot:
Virtue, these days, makes no rich men of us!

The Perfect Couple

Each one a wretch, each one a debauchee;
You, the worst husband, you, the worst of wives:
 Clearly one is surprised to see
That, as good friends, you cannot live your lives.

Sur Chloé

La célèbre Chloé, veuve de sept maris.
      Sous un seul marbre tumulaire,
      Un jour les a tous réunis;
      Puis, elle écrivit sur la pierre:
      C'est moi qui les ai tous mis là.
      Peut-on mieux dire que cela!

De Chloe

Inscripsit tumulo septem scelerata virorum
    "Se fecisse" Chloe, quid pote simplicius?

(Martial IX.15)

A Milon

Milon vend des parfums, des perles, de l'argent,
    Que l'acheteur emporte en s'en allant;
      Mais sa meilleure marchandise
      Est celle de sa femme Lise;
      D'un débit toujours si certain,
      Et qui vendue et revendue
      Jamais pourtant ne diminue,
      Et toujours reste au magasin.

Ad Milonem[a]

Thura, piper, vestes, argentum, pallia, gemmas
    Vendere, Milo, soles, cum quibus emptor abit.
Conjugis utilior merx est, quæ, vendita sæpe,
    Vendentem nunquam deserit, aut minuit.

(Martial XII.102)

---

a. *This epigram is no longer attributed to Martial.*

On Chloe

Widow of seven mates, notorious,
    Chloe decided that one tomb
    Should house them all, concerning whom
    She writ upon the gravestone thus:
    "'Tis I who buried them hereat."
    Can one aught better boast than that!

For Milo

Milo, with silver, pearls, and fragrant scents,
    His eager clientele contents:
    Off they go, satisfied with what
    Delights he has to sell them; but
    Best of his wares is Lise, his spouse:
    Though sold, resold, with much success,
    Never the merchandise grows less,
    Nor need it ever leave the house.

Le Lutteur

A l'heureux vainqueur je préfère
Le vaincu qui, couché par terre,
S'écrie, en bravant le trépas:
"Je meurs, mais je ne me rends pas."

Palæstrita

Non amo qui vincit, sed qui succumbere novit
Et dicit melius τὴν ἐπικλινοπάλην

(Martial XIV.201)

The Wrestler

More than the victor, I prefer
The vanquished, who—defeat, his lot—
Laid low, yet, braving death, cries: "Sir,
I die, but I surrender not."

Les Deux Lapins

Près d'un bois d'Epire,
Suivi d'un mâtin,
(Courait... c'est peu dire)
Volait un lapin.

D'un trou sur la route
Sort un compagnon,
Qui lui dit: Ecoute,
Ami, qu'as-tu donc?

Qui cause ma peine?
Ne le vois-tu pas?
Je suis hors d'haleine...
Un chien suit mes pas.

Je le vois, j'espère!
Mais c'est un limier,
Que tu prends, mon frère,
Pour un lévrier.

Stephen Bernard (1792–1872)

What little we know of Stephen Bernard comes to us via Ruby Van Allen Caulfeild's *French Literature of Louisiana*. Bernard was born in La Rochelle, France. After serving in the French navy, he migrated to Boston in 1824 and eventually settled in Louisiana. In 1848 Bernard was the head of a boarding school in St. Martinville, and he also taught in Shreveport. Eventually settling in New Orleans, Bernard became the head of a private school for boys. He died in New Orleans in 1872.

Stephen Bernard's poetry appeared in the newspaper *Renaissance louisianaise* and the journal *Comptes-rendus de l'Athénée louisianais*. Bernard also wrote three French grammar textbooks, all published between 1832 and 1837. "The Two Rabbits" was first published in *Renaissance louisianaise* in 1867 and republished in *Comptes-rendus* in 1897.

The Two Rabbits[a]

Running—rather, flying!—
A Greek woodland rabbit
Flees a mastiff, trying
From behind to nab it.

From a hole, a chum,
At its pitter-patter,
Comes out, and, "Come, come,"
Queries, "what's the matter?"

"Why, so breathless, am I
In the state you find me?
Don't you see? Look! Damn! I
Have a hound behind me!"

"Certainly I do!
It's a bloodhound, brother!
Not a greyhound!... You
Take one for the other...

Limier, je t'assure,
Comme mon aïeul:
Lévrier, je jure;
Car, moi, j'ai bon œil.

La peur te dirige,
Répond le premier:
C'est limier, te dis-je.
—Non, non, lévrier.

Pendant la dispute
Le chien vint près d'eux,
Et dans la minute,
Les mangea tous deux.

Jeunesse volage.
Sans trop caqueter,
De votre bel âge
Sachez profiter.

"Bloodhound, I'll be bound!
My race knows them well..."
"No! Not *blood*... *Grey*hound!
My sharp eyes can tell!"

"Fear makes you see what
It would have you see.
It's a bloodhound!" "But..."
Their dispute flowed free.

But neither would win it;
For the hound soon followed,
And, in just a minute,
Both of them had swallowed.

Be less chattersome,
Flighty popinjays:
Learn to profit from
Your fair salad days.

---

a. This is based on a fable by Tomás de Iriarte (1750–91),
   Spanish poet and fabulist.

Au printemps

Tendre Printemps, viens rendre à la Nature
Et ses trésors et ses puissants attraits.
Pour te fêter, assis sur la verdure,
Les troubadours chanteront tes bienfaits.

Sous des berceaux de myrtes et de roses,
Tu m'entendras, charmé de ton retour,
A ma Cloé dire de douces choses;
Tu me verras tout rayonnant d'amour.

Tous les amans, dans leurs chansons nouvelles,
Te salûront sous des toits frais et verts;
Sur les bosquets, tous les oiseaux fidèles,
S'assembleront pour former leurs concerts.

Viens donc, accours, la Nature en souffrance,
Du sombre Hiver subit les dures lois!
Elle soupire, implore ta présence;
Elle gémit... n'entends-tu pas sa voix?

Louis Boise

Although the exact dates of Louis Boise's birth and death are unknown, Rodolphe Desdunes's *Our People and Our History* says that he was born, raised, and died in New Orleans. Boise made his living as a tailor, and legend has it that he learned to read only as an adult. Along with his brother Jean, Louis Boise was one of the seventeen Creoles of color who contributed poems to the 1845 anthology *Les Cenelles*. The lyrical "To Spring" is the only poem he ever published.

To Spring

Come, gentle Springtime, and to Nature tender
Once more her charms alluring and her treasures.
The minstrels, singing on the grass, will render
Homage and praise for all your boons and pleasures.

Enchanted shall I lie; and you will hear—
With rose and myrtle boughs swaying above—
The words I whisper to my Chloë dear,
And see me, beaming, radiant with love.

To welcome you, each beau's voice will be heard
Singing new songs beneath the cool, green cover;
And woodland groves will echo as each bird
Warbles his tune, ever your loyal lover.

So come! Make haste!... Waste not your time, dear Spring!
In Winter's grip, distress is Nature's lot!
She begs you come allay her suffering...
She groans, she moans... What? Can you hear her not?

Le Chêne et le Roseau

Ain jour gros Chêne dit ti Roseau:
To plis piti qu'ain ti zozo,
Ain ti di vent, pas plis, ma chère
Capab d'ain cou fou toi par terre.

To bien hardi, gros n'harbe cochon,
To gros, mais faib comme ain mouton,
Attende di vent, ta oir, ma chère,
Qui moun qui va coucher par terre.

Di vent vini, di vent soufflé,
Et tout d'ain coup li rédoublé;
  Tchombo, roseau!...
  Roseau tchombo,
  Mais pour gros chêne
  Qui dans la plaine
  So feilles parti
  Li tout-tout ni.

MORALE

Pas fait gros vente, ain jour ta vini plat;
Gros papa lion ça peur ain ti dérat.

Jules Choppin (1830–1914)

Jules Choppin was born in Louisiana's Saint James Parish in 1830.
Choppin was a first-generation Creole in that both his parents were
French immigrants. Choppin attended Georgetown College, later teaching
Greek and Latin there. Eventually he returned to New Orleans and joined the
faculty at Tulane University as a professor of French language and literature.
Between 1896 and 1905 Choppin published approximately thirty-six poems
and verse fables in *Comptes-rendus de l'Athénée louisianais*. Told in a black
Creole dialect, "The Oyster and the Adversaries" was first published in
Comptes-rendus in 1898; "The Hare and the Tortoise" appeared in 1902.

The Oak and the Reed

One day fat oak, him stand and talk
To little reed: "Wind come, go 'awk!'
You just like bird, so you know what?
Breeze blow, him knock you on you butt!"

Reed, him say: "You brave, like fat pig,
But weak like lamb! Who care how big?
You wait... Wind come and, you know what?
We go see who fall flat on butt!"

Wind, him come blow and, not too long,
Sudden, him go blow twice as strong:
      Hold on, poor reed!...
      Poor reed hold on...
      Oak, him concede,
      All nice leaves gone,
      And him, lie there
      All bare, all bare.

MORAL

Don't go make boast, one day you go lay flat:
Big papa lion, him scared of little rat.

L'Huître et Les Plaideurs

Dé n'hommes tapé promnain, ain jou, au bord la mer.
Yé tous les dés ensembe oi ain dézouite parter.
Ain dans yé happé li, et dit c'était pou li…
L'aute la té si colère qué li talé fou li,
Mais jige la galopé pou péché yé té bat,
Pasqué dé n'hommes léyé té là comme chien et chat.
Et li dit yé: "Ouzaute sorti trouvé dézouite,
Attende, et ma dit vous pou qui li yé… tout souite."
Li ouvri dézouite la et pis li calé li;
Et pis li dit: comme moin c'est jige, mo valé li.
Et pis pou pas vou cré qué moin c'est ain canaille,
Mapé donne vous chacaine ain joli ti lécaille.

MORALE

Si tolé dispité pas couri côté jige,
Pasqué ya oté toi jisqu'à to vié chimige.
Tout ça to capab fait yé va dit to coupab;
Vaut mié to paix, et pis… débate comme to capab.

Le Lièvre et la Tortue

Raconté par "Pa Guitin"

Ain jou, compère Lapin et pis madame Torti
Lévé avant soleil. Yé té jonglé sorti
Pou cou assise au ras chimin pou yé posé,
Et comme dé vié zamis yé commencé causé.
Torti la dit Lapin: "Qui ça tolé parié
Ma rendi côté bit dans grand chimin, prémier?"
Lapin la parti ri et dit Torti: "To fou…
Pou qui to prend Lapin, vié barbotère la boue?"
Torti réponde: "An-hant, to per parié toujou…
To jis conain 'jonglé' o-bin mangé di chou."
"A-bin, 'top,' ma parié," Lapin la dit…" Coupez…"
Et Torti la parti. Lapin la cou coucher,
Et pis sauter, danser, et berdasser longtemps.
Li té si sir gaingnain qué li té prend so temps,
Mais vié madame Torti marché *goudou, goudou,*
Pendant qué ti Lapin taé jouer comme ain ti fou;

The Oyster and the Adversaries

Two friend go walk one day by water, see
Oyster on ground, same time... One say: "That be
For me!" and go make grab... Other, him so
Angry, him say: "Oh?" Ready come to blow...
Then judge come by, run up, and him say: "Drat!
No need you two go fight like dog and cat!
Me know you just find oyster. But do better
Wait, and me tell you who, which one go get her..."
Then him crack oyster, swallow, one two three,
And say: "Me judge, so oyster be for me!
But no want you think me damn snake from hell,
So here! Me give each one nice oyster shell."

MORAL

Never ask judge decide! Judge all got knack:
Take everything, steal old shirt off your back!
Always you lose, no matter what. So then,
Better make peace... Later, go fight again.

The Hare and the Tortoise

Told by "Pa Guitin"

One day, before sun up, friend Rabbit come
Join Madame Turtle. Them decide, by gum,
Better them stay by path, poke round a bit,
Take easy. Them old friend, and so go sit,
Have chat... Turtle she say to Rabbit: "See?
Little hill there, on road? Who bet—you, me,
Go race—me get there first!" "Ha ha! Ho ho!"
Rabbit him laugh. "You crazy so-and-so!
Lazy old stick-in-mud! Me rabbit! Bah!
What you think rabbit do?" Turtle say: "Ha!
You scare you lose! You only good for play,
And for go nibble cabbage every day!"
"Oh?" Rabbit answer. "Good! Me bet!... You start!..."
So Turtle she begin... Rabbit him dart
Back, forth... Lie down, take nap... Get up, no hurry...
Jump, dance, do jig... Take plenty time... No worry,

Et *zing* lapin parti, mais li parti trop tard,
Et dans la monte Torti, Lapin té en rétard.

MORALE

Zamis, coutez moin bien: quand volé fait quichoge
Faut vos lévé bonne her, et pis couté l'horloge...
Sitôt li sonain *ting*... bardez, zamis, parti...
Va fait, pas comme Lapin, mais comme madame Torti.

Know easy him go win!... Turtle she walk
While silly Rabbit play... *Plok plok, plok plok...*
Then *whish!*... Him start up... Fly... Reach hill... Too late!
Turtle already there, just sit and wait!

MORAL

Me give advice, friend. You got stuff to do?
When clock go off—*dring dring!*—you go off too!
If chance come for you win, better you grab it:
Go do like Madame Turtle, no like Rabbit.

Vers Ecrits sur l'Album de Mademoiselle * * *

L'étoile qui scintille en la voûte des cieux,
De l'astre de la nuit la suave lumière
Sont moins douces à voir qu'un regard de tes yeux
      Sous ta brune paupière.

Les Aveux[a]

ROMANCE

Je ne t'ai jamais dit: je t'aime,
Ces mots à prononcer si doux!
Craignant que mon amour extrême
Soudain ne te mît en courroux;
Mais à te plaire si j'aspire,
Si je brûle de mille feux,
Si ma bouche n'ose le dire,
Ne le vois-tu pas dans mes yeux?

Pierre Dalcour (1813–?)

Pierre Dalcour, a free man of color, was born in New Orleans in 1813 to Pedro Dalcour and Eulalie Allain, both free Creoles of color. Early on Dalcour's father sent him to Paris, where he was raised and educated. Pierre Dalcour returned to New Orleans as an adult, but he found the daily reminders of American racism intolerable and soon moved back to Paris. Along with the playwright Victor Séjour and the poet Camille Thierry, also Creoles of color from New Orleans, Dalcour enjoyed access to literary circles frequented by Alexandre Dumas père. Pierre Dalcour contributed twelve poems to the anthology *Les Cenelles;* these poems, which were written during a visit to New Orleans, constitute the sum of his published work. Because he considered Dalcour to be one of the best poets represented in *Les Cenelles,* Armand Lanusse, the anthology's editor, used two of his poems to begin and end the collection. Pierre Dalcour died in Paris, although the exact date is unknown.

Lines Written in the Album of Mademoiselle * * *

The star that twinkles high in heaven's expanse,
The moonlight, gentle, in the darkening skies,
Are not so sweet to look on as a glance
    From your brown-lidded eyes.

Declaration

ROMANCE

I never said to you those sweet
And tender words: "I love you," lest,
Plying a passion indiscreet,
I raise the wrath within your breast;
But if I yearn to please you so,
If fire my silent tongue belies,
If my lips dare not tell you, oh!
Can you not see it in my eyes?

Le regard, mieux que la parole,
Exprime un tendre sentiment,
Pour dire j'aime, ô ma créole,
Le regard est plus éloquent;
Auprès de toi quand je soupire
Et demeure silencieux,
Ce que ma bouche n'ose dire
Ne le vois-tu pas dans mes yeux?

Mais tu feins de ne pas comprendre
Ce que mes yeux t'ont dit souvent,
Et ce que d'amour le plus tendre
Peut renfermer un cœur aimant.
Cruelle, toujours je désire
Et n'ose t'exprimer mes vœux;
Ce que ma bouche craint de dire
Ne le vois-tu pas dans mes yeux?

Toujours ta voix enchanteresse
Vient porter le trouble en mes sens;
Je t'aime, hélas, avec ivresse,
Toi qui causes tous mes tourmens!
Oh! mais je t'aime avec délire,
Aujourd'hui reçois mes aveux:
Enfin ma bouche ose te dire
Ce que cent fois t'ont dit mes yeux.

---

a. The poem was set to the tune of "J'aime
   se dit par habitude."

The glance, more than the voice, can tell
How deep the lover's sentiments:
To say "I love you," Creole belle,
Greater the glance's eloquence.
So, mute my voice remains, although
Many my loving, soulful sighs:
What my lips dare not tell you, oh!
Can you not see it in my eyes?

But you feign not to understand
What my eyes murmur, uncontrolled;
Cruel one! I place at your command
All of the love my heart can hold.
Ah, yes! I burn for you; but no,
Naught dare I say in common wise;
What my lips fear to tell you, oh!
Can you not see it in my eyes?

Your voice enchants me: powerless
Am I... My sense, my wit, distraught...
Say it I must: I love you! Yes!...
You who have all my torments wrought!
Ah, love! You lay my reason low.
Today, no "ifs", no "buts", no "whys"...
At last, my lips dare tell you, oh!
What said a hundred times my eyes.

Joseph Déjacque (1822–ca. 1865)

One of the most radical of the French émigrés to come to New Orleans, Joseph Déjacque was born in Paris in 1822. His mother was a widow who, to support and educate her son, worked as a laundress. Déjacque's modest beginnings made the socialist ideas of Proudhon and Marx irresistible. As an adolescent he was apprenticed to a house painter. During the Revolution of 1848, Déjacque joined the failed workers' revolt and was banned from Paris. In 1851 he published *Les Lazaréennes,* a collection of incendiary antigovernment poems and fables. He was immediately arrested and sentenced to a two-year prison term but fled the country, going first to Belgium and then to England. By 1854 Déjacque was in New York, where he continued to speak and publish on radical socialist issues, including the abolition of slavery and capitalism. In 1857 he went to New Orleans, where he published an expanded version of *Les Lazaréennes.* In the preface to this edition, Déjacque indicated that many of these poems had been published in Paris but that circulation of the volume had been banned; in fact, the government ordered all copies of this text destroyed.

Frustrated with the apparent complacency of other French exiles and ap-

Lazare, c'est le pauvre, anonyme existence,
Le souffreteux qui heurte au seuil de l'opulence,
L'affamé qui réclame une place au festin
Où le riche s'assied égoïste et hautain.

Lazare c'est le spectre agitant son suaire,
    Le grand déshérité
Qui se dresse du fond de sa froide misère
    Et crie: "EGALITE!"...

palled by slavery and Creole society, Déjacque returned to New York, where he struggled to publish his own newspaper, *Libertaire, journal du mouvement social*. In the summer of 1858 he published two articles outlining why he had left New Orleans. In these essays he blasts slave owners and slavery's apologists and calls for an armed insurrection. Not surprisingly, authorities blocked the distribution of these issues. Déjacque's parting shots at the American South were published in *Libertaire* under the rubric "The Liberation of Black Americans." Three articles were devoted to John Brown's rebellion, abolition, and the need for social and economic revolution. It is doubtful that the Creoles of New Orleans were either surprised or sorry to learn of Déjacque's death, in a Paris hospital for the mentally disturbed, circa 1865.[1]

---

1. Joseph Déjacque, *A bas les chefs!* ed. and intro. Valentin Pelosse (Mensil: Editions Champ Libre, 1971), 11–28. This edition includes "La Question Révolutionnaire," "L'Humanisphère," and "La Libération des noirs américains." Pelosse states that Déjacque died in 1864, but Auguste Viatte indicates that the year of death was 1865 ("Complément à la bibliographie louisianaise de Edward Larocque Tinker," *Revue de Louisiane* 3, no. 2 [1974]: 23).

Lazarus is the nameless, sickly pauper
Who, at wealth's doorway, stumbles, comes a cropper;
The starveling who demands to have his place,
And banquet with the rich—vain, haughty race.

Lazarus is the ghost, waving his shroud—
    Disowned, forsaken—he
Who, from his cold woe, stands before the crowd,
    And cries: "Equality!"...

L'Orpheline

Dans son berceau de mousse
L'oiseau le plus petit
Sous l'aile chaude et douce
Douillettement grandit.
La féconde nature,
Veillant sur son destin,
Pourvoit à sa pâture.
Tous ont part au festin!

    Et, sans famille,
    Sur le chemin,
    Moi, pauvre fille,
    Je tends la main!

La fleur qui vient d'éclore
Sous l'horizon vermeil
Brillamment se colore
Aux rayons du soleil.
Sur sa tige flexible
Le zéphyr caressant
De son souffle indicible
La berce en l'embrassant.

    Et, sans famille,
    Sur le chemin,
    Moi, pauvre fille,
    Je tends la main!

Il est de par le monde
Des riches, des heureux,
Pour qui le sort féconde
Tous les fruits savoureux.
Lorsqu'auprès d'eux s'incline
Et veille un ange blond,
La couronne d'épine
Ensanglante mon front!

The Orphan Girl

In its moss cradle-nest,
The bird, small though it be,
By soft, warm wing caressed,
Grows up in luxury.
Nature—lush, provident—
Makes sure the tiny beast
Lacks not for nourishment.
And all join in the feast!

    Orphan am I,
    Poor young waif... And
    To passersby
    Reach out my hand!

The flower that blooms anew,
Afar, as day is done,
Sports the bright crimson hue
Shed by the setting sun.
And, as each zephyr's puff,
Embracing, bends it low,
No words are quite enough
To tell how sweet they blow.

    Orphan I am,
    Poor young waif... And
    To passersby
    Reach out my hand!

Fate casts her fertile favor
On the rich, fortune-rife:
None but the wealthy savor
The tastiest fruits of life.
When guardian angel fair
Gives them a nod and bow,
The crown of thorns I wear
Bloodies my anguished brow!

Et, sans famille,
Sur le chemin,
Moi, pauvre fille,
Je tends la main!

Suresnes, 1851

La Goutte d'Eau

FABLE

L'aurore éclaire l'horizon.
Sur un tissu de fleurs,—rose, lis, ou pensée,—
Comme sur un mol édredon,
Brille une goutte de rosée.
Perle obscure, ignorée, elle a passé la nuit,
Au fond du calice enfermée;
Mais à l'aube elle en sort limpide, parfumée,
Et de l'azur des cieux son cristal resplendit.
—L'apercevant enfin et si claire et si pure,
Le gazon, humide verdure,
—Comme une multitude idolâtre d'amour,—
Se prosterne, et demeure incliné vers la terre
Jusqu'à l'heure où l'astre du jour
De ses rayons de flamme êchauffe l'atmosphère.

—Soulevé par la brise, il cherche alors en vain,
Sa goutte de rosée, idole du matin:
La goutte, au moment même où montait la louange,
Avait roulé de la fleur dans la fange,
Et n'était déjà plus,—ô funeste destin!—
Qu'un immonde mélange...

Publiciste ou tribun: le génie ignoré,
A l'heure où l'univers fléchit devant sa gloire,
N'est plus digne souvent,—grand cœur dégénére,—
Que d'être au poteau de l'histoire
Par le mépris public cloué, déshonoré...

—Comme la goutte d'eau, l'homme est mobile et change:
Le matin, perle pure, et le soir, vile fange...

Londres, 1851

Orphan am I,
Poor young waif... And
To passersby
Reach out my hand!

Suresnes, 1851

The Drop of Water

FABLE

The dawn begins to light the skies,
Above a tapestry of flowers outspread—
   Soft, downy quilt! And on the bed
   Of pansy, lily, rose, there lies,
Sparkling, a dewdrop. Unseen, she had spent
   The night in the obscurity
Of a deep calyx; but, at first light, she
Comes forth again, limpid, with fragrant scent
And crystal-bright in skies' pure blue. Moist-green,
   The grass, who had before not seen
Her beauty, like lovesick idolater—
Vast race!—bows, worships her, head to the ground,
   Until day's heavenly *voyageur,*
With rays of flame heats hot the air all round.

Then, raised up by a breeze, the grass, love-torn,
Sees not his *adorata* of the morn...
Seeks her... In vain!... For she, poor drop, had slipped—
While yet her praise was being paid—and dripped
   Out of the flower (O fate forlorn!):
Now, dew no more, but muck, foul, nondescript...

Orator, journalist... Genius, unknown
When all the universe bows to his glory,
May well deserve, in time—unworthy grown—
   History's scorn, as in our story,
Pilloried by the public, spurned, alone.

Man, like the dewdrop, changes; such, his luck:
Pure pearl at dawn; at dusk, alas, mere muck...

London, 1851

Le Lion

Alors, crinière au vent, sans entrave ni maître,
    L'œil au feu, farouche, indompté,
Il errait au désert sous des cieux de salpêtre,
    Libre au sein de l'immensité...
Et les monts de granit et les plaines de sable
    A ses bonds servaient de tremplin;
Et, comme le clavier d'un orgue formidable,
    Les rauques échos du ravin
De ses rugissements répercutaient l'orage!...
    Depuis, sous le fouet du dompteur,
Docile, il assouplit son allure sauvage,
    Ses fiers instincts, sa mâle ardeur.
Enfin il s'est fait chien; il rampe à tout caprice.
    Cependant, las de tels affronts,
Un jour, il se redresse et son poil se hérisse.
    —Le joug ne sied point aux lions—
Et bientôt sous ses dents il tord, brise, triture
    Et dompteur et verge de fer.
Joie amère!... une cage, oppressive ceinture,
    Le sépare encore du désert!...

Parfois aussi le peuple, à bout de patience,
    Rugit un cri de délivrance.
Mais,—vainqueur politique,—esclave social—
Il retombe énervé, loin du vaste idéal,
Dans sa cage d'abus, de vices, d'ignorance,
    Sous les chaînes du Capital...

Paris, 1851

The Lion

Back then, he roamed the wild's immensity,
    Masterless, fury in his eye,
Mane flying in the wind, unconquered, free,
    Under the hot saltpeter sky...
There, from the granite peaks or plains sand-strewn,
    He would go bounding, undefeated,
And, like a mighty organ's throaty tune,
    Echoes in the ravine repeated
The tempests of his roaring yesterdays...
    But soon, beneath the tamer's lash,
Docile, he left behind his savage ways,
    His proud male instincts, boldly brash,
And he became a lapdog, doing what
    Was pleasing to his master's whim...
One day, however, sick of being the butt
    Of all the vile affronts to him,
He rears up, skin a-crawl, cries: "Yokes are not
    The lion's lot!" And, fangs bared, he
Goes ripping, wrenching, gnashing, on the spot,
    The now powerless enemy,
And mashes to a pulp, there, on the ground,
    Tamer despised, and lash no less...
Ah, bitter joy!... A cage still hems him round,
    Far from his savage wilderness!

Ofttimes, the masses, too, their patience sated,
    Roar free, no longer subjugated.
But though political their victory,
Social slaves, they, encaged in infamy,
Far from their goal remain, flayed, thankless, hated,
    Enchained Capitalistically...

    Paris, 1851

Le Ténia

Entre les mains des vieux docteurs
A qui l'humanité doit tant de funérailles.
Un homme, hélas! se tord sous d'atroces douleurs:
Un ver, le ténia, lui ronge les entrailles.
En vain prodigue-t-il et le lait et le miel.
 A son avide parasite.
A peine a-t-il fini, que celui-ci s'agite
 Plus fort, plus ardent, plus cruel.
Et cherche à perforer son cœur d'un coup mortel.

—Un savant vient et dit: "Laisse là le laitage
"Et tout ce qui nourrit le mal dont tu te plains.
 "Crois-moi, bois cet amer breuvage,
"Il contient pour les vers des poisons souverains."
Le souffrant prend le bol, le vide; et le vampire
Dans les convulsions presque aussitôt expire.

 Il est aussi pour le corps social
Un ténia rongeur, parasite infernal,
Qui, de ses longs anneaux déroulant le cortège,
 Dans son immense torsion,
 Enlace la production:
 Ce monstre, c'est le privilège.
Pour l'expulser du sein de la société,
Ce qu'il faut, ce n'est point choses édulcorées,
Mais des mépris amers, des haines acérées,
Mais le droit dans sa force et sa rigidité.

La Bûche et la Scie

Sous une dent d'acier une bûche gisait
 Et gémissait.
 A la morsure de la scie
Ne sachant qu'opposer sa force d'inertie,

The Tapeworm

FABLE

Cared for by the old doctors whom
 Humanity can thank for giving
So many of its numbers to the tomb,
A man lies writhing: in his belly, living,
A tapeworm gnaws and gorges on his gut.
In vain he plies the avid parasite
 With dose of milk and honey; but,
Quick to consume, at once its appetite
Returns, still keener, and more cruelly it
Slithers, nibbling his heart through, bit by bit.

A man of science comes and tells him: "You
Nourish your ill, my friend. You merely feed it!
 Believe me, drink this bitter brew,
The perfect poison for all worms." Indeed, it
Is, and he gulps it down... Almost as fast,
The vampire in his flesh writhes, gasps its last.

 The body social has as well
Its tapeworm—hungry parasite from hell!—
That, with its great and twisting coils—ah, shame!—
 Upon the body basely loosed,
 Strangles all that it has produced.
 "Privilege" is the monster's name.
To cast it straightway from the social breast,
We need not measures of the pleasantest,
But bitter scorn, and hatreds fury-eyed,
And rigid force of law, rightly applied.

The Log and the Saw

FABLE

A log there was that, moaning, lay beneath
 Steel teeth.
 Groaning, as into it
The saw, with no resistance, bit and bit,

Et sur le chevalet réduite à demeurer,
      Elle se sent,—douleur mortelle,—
      De l'écorce jusqu'à la moëlle,
Par le tranchant aigu meurtrir et déchirer.

Que la lame d'acier, sceptre de l'Arbitraire,
Déchire en se jouant ou ta chair ou tes droits,
Comme l'inerte bûche,—ô honte!—que de fois,
Gisant et gémissant, Peuple, tu laissas faire!...

  Paris, 1852

A Madame F. B.

  (A Bruxelles)

Sous les cieux de l'exil,—et comme l'hirondelle,—
      Au vent de la proscription
Je fuyais, frêle et nu, pauvre et battant de l'aile,
      De nation en nation.
A mon passage alors, Providence angélique,
      Emiettant le pain de l'espoir,
Vous m'avez caressé d'une voix sympathique;
      Votre or a lui dans mon ciel noir.
Un nuage a passé sur l'or; mais j'ai de l'âme
      Gardé l'accent consolateur.
Et ce doux souvenir je le couve, Madame,
      Au tendre duvet de mon cœur.

  New York, 1854

Brune ou Blonde?

Est-elle brune? est-elle blonde?
—L'amour est aveugle en ce monde.—
Elle est brune, disent les uns.
—Que ses cheveux soient blonds ou bruns,
Qu'importe! si, sur son visage,
L'auréole de la beauté,
Eblouissante de clarté,
Opère à mes yeux ce mirage.

  Nouvelle-Orléans, février 1856

The log, in its inert passivity,
    Aching from bark to marrow, quite
    Still, at the sharp blade's every bite,
Did naught to ease its deathly misery.

How often, like the log, O People, you
Let the steel scepter of Rule Arbitrary
Hack at your flesh, your rights—ah, shame!—unwary,
And let be done to you what one would do!

    Paris, 1852

For Madame F. B.

In Brussels

Swallow-like, underneath an exile sky,
    Blown on the winds of banishment,
I fled—poor, naked, frail—and I would fly
    From land to land. And, as I went
My way, angelic Providence would strew
    A few fair crumbs of hopefulness,
And with a voice of sweet compassion, you
    Embraced me in its warm caress.
Your gold lit my dark sky... But though that gold
    Is dimmed now by a cloud, yet am
I ever, by your soul's refrain consoled—
    And memory soothes my heart, Madame.

    New York, 1854

Brunette or Blonde?

Is she a blonde or a brunette?
Love is blind in this world. And yet,
Some say her hair is brown, some say
Her hair is blond. But, come what may,
What matters it in either wise,
So long as, with radiance divine,
The halo of her beauty shine
And grant this vision to my eyes!

    New Orleans, February 1856

De Trouverre[a] à Souveraine

Pour ceindre votre front,
D'autres vous donneront
Guirlandes argentines,
Tresses de perles fines,
Boutons d'or entr'ouverts...
Moi, pour joyau de femme,
Je n'ai rien que des vers,
C'est-à-dire, mon âme...

Nouvelle-Orléans, 1ᵉʳ mai 1856

---

a. In all probability, the misspelling of *trouvère*
as *trouverre* was the printer's error.

L'Huître et la Perle

FABLE

Loin de l'enivrement et de l'éclat des fêtes,
   Au fond du livide Océan,
Une Perle dormait à l'abri des tempêtes:
Une Huître et sa coquille était tout son roman.

Que de femmes aussi, que de perles sans nombre,
Dans la société, ce gouffre amer et sombre,
Et loin des purs rayons d'un amour libre et doux,
Sont captives au sein de l'immonde coquille
   Qu'on nomme la famille,
Et n'ont pour horizon qu'une huître, leur époux!

Nouvelle-Orléans, janvier 1857

The Troubadour to His Queen

Some will your brow entwine
With silvered garlands fine,
Richly enwreathing it
With pearls most exquisite,
Golden buds, opening...
But, for your diadem,
Naught but my verse I bring:
My soul, my only gem...

New Orleans, May 1, 1856

The Oyster and the Pearl

FABLE

Far from life's heady, festive feasts, asleep—
    As roundabout the tempest swirled—
A Pearl lay in the Ocean's pallor deep:
An Oyster and its shell were all her world.

How many women, too, are pearls, like this,
Trapped in society's somber abyss—
Far from the pure rays of love chosen, free—
Who, loveless, must endure a captive fate
    In the foul shell called "family,"
Whose whole world is, alas, their oyster-mate!

New Orleans, January 1857

La Guêpe et l'Abeille

La Guêpe, un jour, rencontrant une Abeille,
   Lui dit: Ma sœur, mais c'est vraiment merveille
Qu'on taise mon mérite et qu'on prône le tien!
Nous avons le même air et le même maintien:
   Ailes et dards, tout est même nature.
Oui, tout, lui dit l'Abeille, excepté la piqûre.
Dans celle que je fais, pour calmer la douleur
Je verse un peu de miel... tu n'es donc pas ma sœur!

Charles-Chauvin-Boisclair Deléry

(1815–80)

Charles-Chauvin-Boisclair Deléry was born into an old, wealthy Creole family in St. Charles Parish in 1815. At fourteen he was sent to Paris to study at the Lycée Louis-le-Grand, where many Creoles educated their sons. Eventually Deléry entered and completed medical school in Paris, and in 1842 he returned to New Orleans to practice medicine. He was a prolific writer whose publications included essays on political philosophy, yellow fever, slavery, the Civil War, and the death penalty. Believing that the South was unprepared for such a war, Deléry was initially against secession from the Union. When New Orleans was captured in 1862, Deléry wrote criticisms of the occupying Union army so scathing that no newspaper editor dared publish them. His opinions became so well known, however, that General Butler ordered his arrest in 1863. The doctor's friends quickly spirited him out of New Orleans to Cuba and then to France, where he spent the rest of the war.

During Reconstruction Deléry's attacks on the local and federal governments became even more vitriolic. In poetry, drama, and prose his became the voice of the old social order refusing to concede defeat. In 1877 Charles Deléry wrote *L'Ecole du peuple,* a drama satirizing the administration of Lieutenant Governor P. B. S. Pinchback, a man of color. (Pinchback was the grandfather of the Harlem Renaissance writer Jean Toomer.) Production of the play was prohibited in New Orleans. Deléry died in 1880. These poems appeared in *Comptes-rendus* on Oct. 1, 1911.

The Wasp and the Bee

A wasp, one day, chancing to meet a bee,
Tells her: "My sister, it amazes me
That they who praise your worth never proclaim
My own, though we, in mien, are much the same:
All of one nature, like in dart and wing."
"Yes," says the bee, but different in the sting.
When I give mine, I soothe the burning blister
With honeyed droplets... No, you're not my sister!"

L'Arbre et le Mât

Un Arbre dit un jour au Mât:
Combien j'ai sur toi d'avantage!
Je protège de mon ombrage
Et l'homme, et les troupeaux, des ardeurs du climat.
C'est sous mon dôme vert qu'on danse, qu'on se fête;
Et c'est là que l'oiseau, plein de joie et d'amour,
Court saluer l'aurore; à son tour, le poète
Y vient pour respirer ses chants de troubadour.
Mais, toi, pauvre bois mort, inutile cadavre,
On te voit, languissant dans ton oisiveté,
Tendre au ciel ton front chauve, et pourrir dans un havre,
Pour être, par les vers, plus tard, déchiqueté.
Mais aussi, quelle idée eus-tu jamais, mon frère,
De troquer nos jardins contre ce cimetière?
Quel profit tires-tu d'un choix aussi mauvais?
Je suis *self made man,* moi, comme dit l'Anglais.
Or, pendant qu'à l'envi le monde me recherche,
On te laisse à l'écart, ma pauvre grande perche!
—Très bien dit, mon cousin, car nous sommes cousins,
Non frères, s'il vous plaît: La famille des pins,
Par sa taille élancée, et sa haute stature,
A l'honneur de fournir aux vaisseaux leur mâture.
D'ailleurs, qu'il t'en souvienne, ainsi que toi je fus
Un arbre; il est très vrai que tes rameaux touffus
Abritent quelquefois des moutons, ou des vaches,
Quelques grands fainéants, des troubadours ganaches.
Le beau mérite! Un drap pourrait en faire autant
Pour peu qu'on le déplie et qu'on le tende au vent.
Mais moi, morbleu, mon cher, je suis un autre sire.
Je n'abrite, il est vrai, moutons ni troubadours;
Mais je fais, sur les flots, voltiger ce navire;
Sur place il pourrirait sans mon puissant concours.
Tu me crois un oisif! J'admire ta faconde;
Sais-tu bien que trois fois j'ai fait le tour du monde?
Les hommes vont à toi; je vais au-devant d'eux:
Qui donc, tout bien pesé, les sert mieux de nous deux?
De la vague en fureur je nargue la colère;
Mon front armé d'acier repousse le tonnerre.
Des humains, chaque jour, je porte les destins;

The Tree and the Mast

A tree, one day, said to a mast:
"Far worthier am I, friend, than you!
My thick leaves shelter all those who—
Man, beast—seek refuge from the stifling blast,
The summer's heat. Beneath my canopy
Of green, they dance, and feast, and gaily fete
Their joy; and there the bird, in revelry
Of love, welcomes the dawn; disconsolate,
There, too, the poet sighs his sighs; whereas
You, lifeless wood... Of what good, of what value
Are you, poor idle corpse? What virtue has
That brow of yours, stripped bare? By and by shall you—
Rotting in port, while reaching for the sky—
Stand, worm-defaced perhaps! But tell me, why,
My brother, you ill chose to give up our
Flowering woodland grove, our garden bower,
For such a graveyard! I, at least, can say
I am, myself, a 'self-made man,' as they
Put it in English... And, while everyone
Comes after me, nobody, brother, none
Goes seeking you, miserable pole!" "Well said,
Cousin!... Yes, 'cousin,' if you please, instead
Of 'brother'... For, cousins indeed are we:
The tall and slender pinetree family
Provides—and it is honored so to do!—
Boats' timbers, with broad sails affixed thereto.
Besides, remember that I was, no less
Than you, a tree. Ah yes, it's true, I guess,
That your thick, leafy limbs shelter, at times,
Sheep, cows, and poets blathering their rhymes.
So what? A sheet could do as much if it
Were held, unfurled, against the wind a bit!
I, damn it! am a different sort, *mon cher*.
True, I protect no sheep, cows, troubadours,
Or shelter any other folk of yours.
But, thanks to me, this fleet boat rends the air,
Flitting over the waves. Without my help,
My strength, it would stand rotting... Blithering whelp!
I much admire your well-hung tongue! You take

Que deviendraient, sans moi, tous ces pauvres marins?
Grâce à moi, ce navire, aux lointaines contrées
Porte des voyageurs, et toutes ces denrées,
Qui vont alimenter des peuples affamés;
A peine entrés au port, nous sommes acclamés.
Au profit des humains, j'affronte les tempêtes;
En somme, moi, je vis, lorsque, toi, tu végètes.
Avant donc sur mon sort de geindre et de gémir,
Va, crois-moi, cher cousin, te faire dégrossir.

Me for an idler, do you? Well, you make
A fell mistake! A full three trips I've made
Around the globe... And though men seek your shade,
And come to you, I go to them! Now, which
One of us fills the more important niche
In man's existence? I defy the waves'
Harsh clash; my steel-tipped brow it is that saves
The vessel from the lightning's flash. Each day
I rule man's destiny. What would, I pray,
Become of those poor sailors, were it not
For me? And what of those who sail afar?
And the provisions for all those who are
Hungering—starving!—in their distant lands?
No sooner we touch shore than with their hands
And voices they acclaim us, celebrate!
For mankind's good I brave the storm. Aye, mate,
I live, you merely vegetate!... And so,
Before you wail and whimper at my woe,
Forsooth, be less uncouth: you could well be
More smooth and polished, cousin, just like me!"

Un Soir au Jackson Square

Je suis assez bourgeois, croyez-vous, pour me plaire
A ce tableau touchant du plaisir populaire,
Et l'autre soir encore, j'étais, après dîner,
Venu, tout seul, parmi ces gueux, me promener.

Tout en laissant renaître au fond de ma pensée,
Le rêve d'une joie encore ineffacée
Par dix ans de labeur et de déceptions,
Je confondais, parmi les chères visions
Des souvenirs, ce gai jardin plein de murmures,
Les jeux d'enfants, les bruits confus sous les ramures,
Et tous ces promeneurs qui devant moi passaient.

Georges Dessommes (1855–1929)

Georges Dessommes was born in New Orleans in 1855. Like many Creoles with adequate means, the Dessommes family moved to Paris in 1860 to escape the Civil War. Following the custom in wealthy Creole families, Georges Dessommes attended the prestigious Lycée Louis-le-Grand in Paris. In 1870, at age fifteen, he returned to New Orleans. He began writing poetry early on, and his first published efforts appeared in *Comptes-rendus de l'Athénée louisianais* in 1876. For the next three decades Dessommes's work appeared in *Comptes-rendus* and *Carillon*. When Charles Bleton began the *Petit Journal* in 1879, Dessommes became one of its principal editors. Perhaps the most modern of the nineteenth-century francophone writers, Dessommes abandoned romanticism and eventually turned to the realism of writers such as Emile Zola. He published his first novel, *Tante Cydette,* in 1888. The novel presents an unsentimental portrait of the insular francophone Creole world at the turn of the century. The growing interest in francophone Louisiana literature led to the reissue of *Tante Cydette* in 2001. First published in *Comptes-rendus* in 1880, "An Evening in Jackson Square" presents, through the eye of the flaneur, the visually rich and varied scenes in an evening in the life of the city. Georges Dessommes died in 1929.

An Evening in Jackson Square

You think me quite bourgeois enough to be
Pleased by this touching people's tapestry
Of ne'er-do-wells... My dinner done, one night,
Alone, I strolled here to enjoy the sight.

As rose again from deep within my thought
The dream, still-dreamt, of joy that ten years fraught
With disillusions, toils, could not erase,
I let my past's dear visions take their place
Here, amidst all the mingling murmurs, all
The happy garden's playful caterwaul
Of children's games, the muttered whispers from

Que de types divers tour à tour paraissaient
Pour se perdre bientôt dans la foule! Un ménage
D'ouvriers, se troublant fort peu du voisinage
D'un ivrogne braillard aux propos insolents;
Quelque nègre, tout fier dans ses pantalons blancs,
Tournant dans ses gros doigts de superbes breloques,
Tandis que des gamins se pâmaient dans leurs loques
En singeant le milord africain; puis c'étaient
Deux ou trois bons vivants très-lancés qui chantaient,
Ou bien l'essaim bavard d'ouvrières, en quête
De galants, et, ma foi,—vous savez—la conquête
Du cœur est douce autant qu'aisée, au mois de Mai,
Lorsque dans la fraîcheur de l'espace embaumé,
Le printemps répand sa pure, sa chaude haleine
Qui fait germer tous les désirs dont l'âme est pleine.

Cependant au milieu des promeneurs joyeux,
D'autres passaient, muets et seuls, de pauvres vieux,
Flétris par la misère et l'exil, sans familles,
Mal vêtus, mais gardant encor sous leurs guenilles
La dignité des jours meilleurs, morts sans retour.
Ce sont de vieux Français; ils font vingt fois le tour
Du jardin, le regard noyé de rêverie,
Heureux de retrouver vaguement la patrie
Dans ces illusions d'un lointain souvenir.
Pauvres gens! tout-à-l'heure il faudra revenir
A la réalité sinistre de la vie;
Mais dans votre âme, au spleen quelques instants ravie,
—Au fond du gite obscur où vous vous abritez,—
Pour cette nuit, malgré la faim, vous emportez
Un éclair d'allégresse, un rayon d'espérance,
Ce rêve inoubliable et sacré de la France.

Under the boughs, and those passers-by come
To stroll... How many! What variety,
Soon lost among the crowd! A family
Of workers, unconcerned that, by their side,
A brawling drunkard cursed and vilified
The lot; a black, white-trousered, proud as he
Could be, with stubby fingers lovingly
Fondling his watch and chain, while, in their rags,
A group of urchins, mischievous young wags,
Convulsed with pleasure, as, catch-as-catch-can,
They stood aping M'lord the African;
Or two, three modish dandies, singing, humming;
Or working girls, a-swarm, a-chatter, coming
In search of beaus... And, goodness knows, in May,
Easy it is, and sweet, to have one's way
With love, when, with the balm-fresh air conspiring,
Spring's warm breath buds to life the soul's desiring.

But others, too, passed by—pathetic, mute—
Family-less, unloved, poor, destitute
Exiles among the strollers gay; and, though
Tattered their dress and worn, still do they show
The dignity of far-off, fairer days,
Now dead and gone... Old Frenchmen, these, their gaze
Drowned in their reverie, pleased to have found,
Ambling about the garden, round and round,
Their homeland's vague, illusive memory.
Proud folk! Soon will life's cold reality
Beckon you back... But at least for tonight
Your souls' ennui has yielded up one bright,
Brief flash of hope, despite your hunger, there,
In that somber and dreary hovel, where
You lie; that hope, despite fell circumstance:
The sacred dream, never forgotten: France!

Souvenirs du Désert

O belle Louisiane, ô vastes cyprières,
Où m'égaraient jadis des courses solitaires;
Où j'allais, tout enfant, ainsi qu'en un saint lieu,
Ouïr, déjà rêveur, la grande voix de Dieu!
Où j'écoutais, ravi, de vagues harmonies;
Où je m'entretenais avec de doux Génies!
O mon ciel d'Occident, d'où tombait autrefois
La poésie en pleurs dans les blonds lis des bois!

Charles-Oscar Dugué (1821–72)

Charles-Oscar Dugué was born in Jefferson Parish in 1821. As an adolescent Dugué was sent to Paris, where he attended the Collège St. Louis. By the time he returned to New Orleans in 1843, he had decided to become a journalist, and by 1850 he was working for the daily *L'Orléanais.* Eventually, however, he decided to study law. He first worked in his father's firm and then opened his own practice. Nevertheless, Dugué's passion was literature, and in 1847 he published his first volume of poetry, *Essais poétiques,* which contained a long poem dedicated to Chateaubriand, whom he greatly admired. In 1852 he published a play in three acts, *Mila; ou, La mort de La Salle,* that recalls, à la Chateaubriand, the death of La Salle.

In 1858 Dugué, who never mastered English, accepted the directorship of Jefferson College, where all instruction was conducted in French. He remained there until 1863, when the Civil War forced the college to close. After the war he obtained employment at the Collège de Dolbear. On a trip to Paris in 1872, Dugué became ill and died. His body was returned to New Orleans, where he was buried.

Between 1842 and 1870 Dugué's uncollected poetry appeared in several New Orleans papers, including *Courrier de la Louisiane* and *Renaissance louisianaise,* and in the journal *Comptes-rendus.* The poems included here are from *Essais poétiques* and vividly evoke specific Louisiana settings, including the breath-taking beauty of its wilderness and the more intimate beauty of a young Choctaw mother.

Memories of the Wilderness

O fair Louisiana! O you vast
Cypress groves where, alone, in days long past,
My footsteps strayed—a dreamer then, although
But a mere lad!—and where I used to go,
As in some holy place, a-wandering, awed,
To listen to the mighty voice of God;
Where I would hear vague harmonies, and let
Myself converse, in sacred tête-à-tête,

Rivages résonnant de doux échos! Vieux fleuve,
Où mon cœur desséché de loin encor s'abreuve,
Où du Chactas encor j'entends le chant lointain!
O charmante patrie, ô sol américain,
Eden de mon enfance, ô pays des Sauvages,
De toi, dans mon exil, j'ai gardé mille images;
Je revois tes lauriers, et tes grands chênes-verts,
Et tes îlots flottants, de longs roseaux couverts;
Je revois l'horizon, avec ses teintes vives
D'argent, de pourpre et d'or illuminant les rives;
Je revois, réfléchi dans les beaux lacs dormants,
Le fantôme allongé de tant d'arbres géants...

Mais pour mon cœur ému quelle touchante scène!
Voici, là, sur la mousse, une jeune indienne,
Tendre fleur des déserts que l'orage et les vents
N'ont point flétrie encor de leurs souffles brûlants.
D'un peuple vierge encore intéressant usage!
A son oreille pend la perle du rivage;
Des plumes de héron, couronnant sa beauté,
Mélangent sa douceur d'une noble fierté;
Sur son sein demi-nu, comme une étoile brille,
Aux derniers feux du jour, une blanche coquille;
Et ses doigts diligents tressent, en latanier,
Pour voiler son beau corps, un chaste tablier!...
Sur la natte de jonc, parmi les fleurs, sommeille
Un enfant nouveau-né que sa tendresse veille;
Le rouge cardinal, le colibri d'azur
Voltigent à l'entour, dans un air frais et pur;
Sur le front de l'enfant un érable à fleur blanche,
Ainsi qu'un éventail, laisse flotter sa branche;
Et le souffle du soir, jouant dans ses cheveux,
Semble lui murmurer ces mots harmonieux:
Dors, dors, charmant enfant, dors paisible en ta couche;
Aux lèvres du jasmin je préfère ta bouche!

1840

With gentle Spirits! O my New World sky,
Where poetry once rained with tearful cry,
Sprinkling the woodland lilies! Echoes soft,
Wafted from the old river's banks, where oft—
And still!—my parched heart drank, and drinks, though long
My journey here; with Choctaw's distant song
Yet in my ear! O Eden undefiled,
Land of the Savage! Still I hold—exiled,
Alas!—my myriad childhood memories,
America! I see your laurel trees,
Your great holm-oaks, your islets that would seem—
Lush with long reeds—afloat along the stream;
I see the sunsets on your fair shores, those
Brilliant silvered-and-crimsoned golden glows;
I see the forest tall—a phantom—creep,
Reflected, on your lakes, lying asleep...

Ah! Now, touching my heart, there, on the grass
And moss, I see a tender Indian lass,
Flower of the wilderness, but faded not,
Nor withered yet by stormwinds, gusting hot;
And, from her ear, embellishing her graces,
A pearl plucked from the strand—this virgin race's
Intriguing wont; and, on her comely head,
Blending her sweetness with a merited
And noble pride, a heron's plumes; and, there,
Starlike, upon her bosom, all but bare,
A white shell, gleaming in the sun's last rays;
And she, with fingers deft, tresses a maze
Of palm fronds, modest, to conceal her flesh!...
On the reed mat, amidst the flowered *crèche,*
A new-born babe lies, sleeps, as tenderly
She keeps her watch; the azure colibri,
The cardinal red, go flitting, fluttering
Overhead, in the pure, fresh air, a-wing;
A white-bloomed maple floats its swaying bough,
Light on the breeze, and fans the infant's brow;
And, in its hair, the dusk's breath, gently playing,
Murmurs, it seems, in words harmonious, saying:
"Sleep, sleep, dear child, may calm your slumber be:
Sweeter than jasmine are your lips to me!"

1840

Ce Qui Me Fait Rêver

C'est un attrait caché dans mille et mille choses
De ce vaste univers; c'est le souffle des roses
Enivrant dans son vol un colibri d'azur;
C'est le rayon tremblant qui tombe d'un ciel pur;
C'est au couchant lointain la trace d'un nuage;
C'est le bruit de la pluie en roulant du feuillage;
C'est la brise[a] du nord qui, sifflant dans nos toits,
Réveille en notre esprit les songes d'autrefois!...

C'est le balancement des chevelures blondes,
Aux pieds de la beauté tombant en molles ondes.
C'est l'amoureux éclat d'un bel et grand œil noir
Qui laisse, après le bal, au cœur un peu d'espoir...

1842

---

a. This should most likely have been *bise,* not *brise.*

Souvenir du Bal

En vain j'ai dit cent fois: tâchons de l'oublier;
En elle ne voyons désormais rien qui charme,
Ni son épaule nue où brille un noir collier,
Ni son regard limpide où scintille une larme,
Ni sa bouche, fruit rose aux blancs pépins d'émail,
Ni sa main agitant son léger éventail;
    Laissons le temps emporter sur son aile
    Jusqu'à son nom, jusqu'à son souvenir!
    Je ne veux rien, non, je ne veux rien d'elle,
    Avec l'amour mon cœur doit en finir!

En vain, de ces discours appuyant ma faiblesse,
J'ai tenté de chasser la forme enchanteresse;
Toujours son grand œil noir vient luire devant moi;
Toujours sur son beau sein, qu'agite un doux émoi,
Je vois le jais lançant mille reflets de flamme,
Et sa bouche sourire, et sur son front son âme
Briller, comme un flambeau d'espérance et de foi!

What Makes Me Dream

It's the charm hidden in a myriad things
Of this vast universe; hummingbirds' wings
Of azure, drunk on roses' breath, lush scent;
The quivering shaft from the pure firmament;
It's the cloud wisps, afar, on sunset eves;
It's the rain's murmur, trickling off the leaves;
It's the northwind, whistling among the beams,
And waking in our souls yesteryear's dreams!...

It's the belles' toss of head, their loveliness's
Cascades of blond and gently falling tresses;
It's the fond spark that love's dark glance lets fall,
Leaving the heart to hope, after the ball...

1842

Memory of the Ball

In vain a hundred times I've said, "Let's try
To put her from my mind, muse not one whit
On tear that sparkles in her limpid eye,
Or shoulder bare, black necklace lighting it,
Or mouth—fruit pink of flesh, white porcelain pips—
Or hand with fan, waved in fair fingertips;
 Let time in wingèd flight bear off
 Her very name, her memory!
 I want no part of her! Enough!
 Enough! My heart must loveless be!"

With these weak words I tried—alas, in vain!—
To chase her form enchanting from my brain.
But still those black eyes flash before me; still
That lovely bosom, quivering to the thrill
Of passion, casts its myriad glints of jet;
I see her smile, and on her brow shines yet
Her soul, torchlike, where hopeful faith yet lingers!

Toujours le noir velours où s'enlace sa taille
Glisse amoureusement sous ma main qui tressaille,
Et toujours, malgré moi, cet ange, ce démon,
Fait passer sur mon sein la flamme ou le frisson.

1843

L'Amour

L'amour! mais sans amour, ô mon Dieu, comment vivre?
Sans un front de quinze ans dont l'aspect nous enivre;
Sans une bouche rose au souris gracieux;
Sans de brillants yeux noirs pour parler à nos yeux;
Sans une douce voix pour emplir notre oreille;
Sans un bras amoureux qui, le soir, sous la treille,
Enlacé toute une heure autour de notre bras,
Comme un lien de fleurs accompagne nos pas;
Sans le bruissement d'une robe de soie,
Enfermant dans ses plis un corps d'ange qui ploie;
Sans amour, ô mon Dieu, qu'est-ce donc que le cœur?
Sans amour, sans amour, où donc est le bonheur?

1843

Jalousie

Un autre, un autre hélas! belle vierge adorée,
Un autre passera près de toi la soirée!
Un autre te verra, parmi tes jeunes sœurs,
Briller, comme la rose auprès des autres fleurs;
Un autre aspirera le souffle de ta bouche;
Un autre de ta voix, qui pénètre et qui touche,
Recueillera l'accent! et moi je serai seul,
Couvert de ma douleur ainsi que d'un linceul;
Et moi, des pleurs amers baigneront mon visage,
Car déjà je n'ai plus de toi que ton image,
Chaste et charmant portrait que me donna ta main,
Et que peut-être aussi tu reprendras demain!...

Oh! Quand ton bras charmant, courbé comme la branche,
Sur un bras étranger s'appuîra dans le bal;
Quand les plis de ta robe, ou bleue, ou rose, ou blanche,

Still that black velvet, wherein is enlaced,
In elegant caress, her comely waist,
Slips lovingly betwixt my trembling fingers;
And still—though, powerless, I try my best—
This angel-demon flames and chills my breast.

1843

Love

Love! Love! Without it, God, how live we thus?
No fifteen-year-old's brow bewitching us;
No pink lips smiling in that gracious wise;
No eyes—black, sparkling—speaking to our eyes;
No voice to fill our ear with sheer delight;
No arm beneath the arbor vines, at night,
For hours on end, pressing, embracing ours
In our stroll, like a twining cord of flowers;
No swish of silken gown, whose folds enclose
An angel's body in her to-and-fros...
Without love, God, what is the heart? Ah yes!
Without love, where, oh where, is happiness?

1843

Jealousy

Another? What? Another shall, alas,
By your side all this gala evening pass?
Another shall it be who sees you there—
Maiden adored!—among your sisters fair,
Shine like a rose midst other blooms; and he—
Another!—shall inhale your breath, and be
The one to glean your touching voice! And I,
Alone, enwrapped in shroudlike love, shall lie;
Soon shall my tears go welling, streaming; for
I have of you a portrait, nothing more—
Chaste gift your hand bestowed!—to soothe my sorrow,
And that your hand may well take back tomorrow!...

When, at the ball, I see your arm alight,
Like a bough, on another's, pressing... Oh!
When in a swirl of pink, or blue, or white,

Voltigeront au vent, alors pense à mon mal!
Pense que, le cœur plein d'amour et de tendresse,
Moi je suis seul ici dans les amers sanglots;
Pense que, dans mon sein nourrissant ma tristesse,
Je sens rouler en moi les pleurs comme les flots.
Et que le désespoir, ainsi qu'une tempête,
Bouleversant mon âme et grondant dans ma tête,
Fait résonner en moi de douloureux échos!...

1843

Le Ver Luisant et la Violette

C'est avec raison
Que sous le gazon
Tu caches ta tête,
Dit le ver luisant,
D'un ton suffisant,
A la violette:
As-tu, comme moi,
Un feu que l'on voit
Briller dans la plaine?
Je suis tout vermeil,
Je suis le soleil
De la nuit sereine.

Ami, dit la fleur,
De cette lueur
Ton âme est trop fière:
Son éclat ne luit
Que lorsque la nuit
Voile la lumière;
Mais, moi, de mon cœur
S'épand une odeur
Qu'on vante et qu'on aime,
Et cet agrément
A chaque moment
Est chez moi le même.

1847

Your gown goes twirling, pray think of my woe!
Think that, with heart by tender love possessed,
Alone am I, here, sobbing bitterly.
Think that I feel, in my grief-nourished breast,
My tears go flowing like the mighty sea,
And that, like creature tempest-buffeted,
My soul, cast down and growling in my head,
Howls its great echoes of my misery!...

    1843

The Firefly and the Violet

"Right you are, alas,
To hide in the grass
And not show your head."
Supercilious,
The proud firefly thus
To the violet said.
"Is the meadow lit
By your fire? Is it
Seen by everyone?
In the night's calm sky
I glow red, for I
Am the evening sun!"

"Friend," the flower replied,
"You take too much pride
In that glow you cast.
You shine not at all
Till night spreads its pall
And day's light is past.
But, from my breast fair,
Rises in the air
My sweet scent, forever
Ready to delight
By both day and night,
Fragrant, changing never."

    1847

Pensée

*A Mme * * **

Suave passagère,
Pensée, ô douce fleur,
Va, sois la messagère
De mon timide cœur.

Près de ma bien-aimée,
Va, fleur, passer tes jours;
Va, tu seras charmée
Près d'elle, mes amours.

Adolphe Duhart (?–1909)

Lélia D——t is the pseudonym employed by Adolphe Duhart, a free man of color who was born in New Orleans between 1835 and 1840 and educated in France. Duhart was a teacher and an active member of the Creoles-of-color literati, who devoted their considerable energy and talents to creating, cultivating, and preserving Louisiana's francophone literature. In his capacity as a poet, a teacher, and later the principal of the Institution Couvent, Adolphe Duhart was an important part of this movement, which included Armand Lanusse and Joanni Questy.

Duhart's poetry was published in *La Tribune de la Nouvelle Orléans* and *La Renaissance louisianaise*. In 1865 *La Tribune* published a short story and a novel by Duhart. "Simple Histoire," a love story between a slave and his mistress, appeared in the March 9–10 issues, and *Trois amours* was published between August 15 and September 3. Duhart's play *Lélia ou la victime du préjugé* was performed at the Théâtre Orléans on June 10, 1866. There is no known extant copy of *Lélia*. Duhart's pseudonym "Lélia" was the name of his deceased daughter. Adolphe Duhart died in 1909.

Included here are poems from *La Tribune de la Nouvelle Orléans* published between 1864 and 1866.

Pansy

For Madame * * *

Pansy, sweet flower, go fly
In gentlest flight; depart,
Fair messenger of my
Bashful and timid heart.

To my belovèd, wend
Your way, dear flower, and bide
With her. My love, go spend
Your days, charmed, by her side.

Dis-lui, ma fleur chérie,
De mon amour discret
La molle rêverie,
L'ineffable secret...

Fidèle confidente,
Oh! va lui dire encore
De mon âme constante
Les brillants rêves d'or.

Quand sa tête rêveuse
Se penchera sur toi,
Fais naître, ô fleur heureuse,
Un doux penser pour moi.

Oh! sois frêle, légère
Et gracieuse fleur,
Sois alors messagère
Des aveux de mon cœur.

Maris Stella

A Mme P. D.

Etoile, pure étoile
Oh! sur les flots amers
Guide ma blanche voile,
Douce étoile des mers.

Hélas! qui va, sans toi, de ma frêle nacelle
Ecarter l'aquilon qui souffle l'ouragan;
Que ta prière au moins, mon étoile fidèle,
La conduise toujours sur l'immense Océan.

Vois, déjà sur les flots mollement balancée,
Ma nacelle dérive, et bientôt sans effort
Par le vent qui fraîchit, vivement élancée,
Elle sillonne l'onde et fuit enfin le port.

Tell her, fair flower, how soft
My musings; you, the token
Of love discreet, that oft
Needs must remain unspoken...

Let her, good friend, be told
Anew how faithfully
My soul, in dreams of gold,
Shines with love's constancy.

And, happy flower, when thus
She nods to you, pray make
A thought rise, amorous
And tender, for my sake.

Ah! Then, frail flower, come fly
In gentlest flight; depart,
Bring me the message nigh:
The yearnings of her heart.

Stella Maris

For Madame P. D.

Star, pure as pure can be,
Over the bitter brine
Guide this white sail of mine,
Gentle star of the sea.

Who, but for you, will keep my fragile barque
From the North wind's tempestuous blast? Ah! May
Your prayer, over the Ocean vast and dark,
Ever, O faithful star, show her the way!

See how she bobs upon the foam; see how
She breaks adrift... Soon, when the chill winds roar,
Rising, blowing her on, her keel will plough
The waves, as, effortless, she quits the shore...

Oh! l'orage, mon Dieu! le ciel rougit, s'allume;
Come un lion blessé la mer roule et bondit;
Ma nacelle se tord sur les flots blancs d'écume,
Et semble s'engloutir dans l'Océan maudit...

. . . .

Voici qu'à l'horizon s'éteint l'ardente flamme;
Le hardi matelot reprend son chant joyeux.
L'ouragan est passé... Maintenant chaque lame
Doucement s'aplanit et réfléchit les cieux!

> Etoile! douce étoile,
> Oh! sur les flots amers
> Guide ma blanche voile,
> Douce étoile des mers.

Sonnet

A Mme Louise de Mortié

Le cantique sacré qu'un ange dit aux cieux,
Les accords des oiseaux quand l'horizon s'irise,
Tous les bruissements que soulève la brise
Dans des bois en son vol léger, capricieux;

Le rire d'un lutin folâtre et gracieux,
Le murmure des eaux que le vent ride et frise,
Et l'accent virginal d'une vierge surprise
A son premier aveu, tendre et délicieux;

Les préludes naïfs d'un amoureux trouvère,
La prière du Christ tombant sur le Calvaire,
Et son cri de pardon exhalé sur la croix,

Et tout ce que le ciel promet quand on l'implore,
Madame, a moins de charme, est moins divin encore,
Pour nos cœurs captivés, que votre douce voix.

Good God! The storm!... Alas! The skies glow red...
The sea bounds, like a wounded lion... It leaps,
Growls, moans... My barque writhes midst the froth outspread,
Sucked down, it seems, in the sea's cursèd deeps!...

. . . .

But look! Soon the horizon's flame grows dim.
The storm is past... The sailor, by and by,
Boldly sings out once more his joyous hymn...
The waves—subsiding, calm—mirror the sky.

> Star, sweet as sweet can be,
> Over the bitter brine
> Guide this white sail of mine,
> Gentle star of the sea.

Sonnet

For Mme Louise de Mortié

The sacred hymn a heavenly angel sings;
The birds' songs, on the far horizon gleaming
Like opal; all the rustlings' whimsy, streaming
Over the woods, on breezes' gentle wings;

A graceful elfin's gleeful frolickings;
The murmur of the waters, windswept, seeming
A mass of curls; voice of a maid caught dreaming
Her virgin love, with tender mutterings;

The naïve pleadings of a troubadour;
Christ's prayer on Calvary; and, even more,
His sigh of pardon from the cross professed;

And heaven's promise when our pent hearts pine...
All these, Madame, charm less, are less divine,
Than your sweet, gentle voice, the loveliest.

Ange du Ciel

A Mlle E. B——n

Vous que tout bas j'appelle en ma prière,
Ange du ciel, rêve du Paradis,
Comme un rayon du divin sanctuaire
Jetez les yeux sur mon cœur solitaire...
Priez pour moi!... car mes jours sont maudits!...

Pour adoucir mon destin triste et sombre,
Ange du ciel, fille aux douces vertus,
Conduisez-moi sur les écueils sans nombre
Jetés, hélas! sur mon chemin dans l'ombre...
Veillez sur moi... car je n'espère plus!...

L'ombre me glace et vainement je pleure;
Mon front pali de la mort est couvert...
Ange du ciel, dans la froide demeure,
Venez parfois prier [pendant] une heure,
Dans le parvis de mon tombeau désert.

Heavenly Angel

For Mlle E. B——n

Heavenly angel, dream of love divine—
You, whom in my low-murmured prayer I praise—
Like a ray beaming from a holy shrine,
Let your glance light this lonely heart of mine...
Pray for me!... For, alas, cursed are my days!

To calm my dismal fate, my dark distress—
Heavenly angel, gracious, virtue-bred—
Guide me amongst the pitfalls numberless
Strewn thick about my path's black emptiness...
Watch over me, for all my hope is fled!

The shadows chill me, and in vain I cry.
My pallid brow is shrouded with death's gloom...
Heavenly angel, may you, by and by,
Come spend an hour, praying here, where I lie:
Here, in the cold, by my abandoned tomb!

Oui et Non

Oui, dans votre bouche divine,
Me semble, Adèle, un nouveau mot:
Mon cœur l'entend ou le devine,
L'Amour et lui sont de complot.
Ne vous en fâchez pas, Adèle,
Laissez-moi mon illusion:
Oui, vous rend mille fois plus belle,
Ah, ne me dites jamais non!

Emilie Poullant de Gelbois Evershed (1800–1879)

Born in Nantes, France, in 1800, Emilie Poullant de Gelbois came to New Orleans as a newlywed between 1817 and 1818. Soon after the birth of their child, her husband abandoned her. In 1824 she married a Mr. Evershed, with whom she had a son. Just two years later her second husband died during an outbreak of yellow fever, which annually decimated the population of New Orleans. To support her children, Evershed taught French and music privately. In the early 1840s Emilie Evershed's poetry began to appear in *L'Abeille,* the *Revue louisianaise,* and *Courrier de la Louisiane.* Evershed published not only thirty-plus poems in these newspapers but also two volumes of poetry, *Essais poétiques* (1843) and *Esquisses poétiques* (1846), and two novels, *Eglantine ou le secret* (1843) and *Une Couronne blanche* (1850). Her brother-in-law provided funds for the publication of these volumes, which were published in Paris.

Evershed is one of just two women poets in this collection, and although her poetry rarely strays from the familiar themes of maidenhood, courtship, marriage, and family, her verse is surprisingly fresh and engaging. "Yes and No" comes from her first volume, *Essais poétiques.* Emilie Evershed died in New Orleans in 1879.

Yes and No

A yes from your mouth heavenly,
Adèle, truly a new word seems.
My heart hears it, faint though it be,
Conspiring with Love in his schemes.
Be not displeased with me, Adèle;
Let my illusions gull me so.
A yes makes you a peerless belle:
I beg you, never tell me no!

Oui, sur vos lèvres adorées
Me semble un son venu des cieux!
Zéphire aux ailes azurées
Le murmure à mon cœur heureux.
Ah, qu'il soit pour moi seul, Adèle,
Pardonnez ce léger soupçon;
Et quand on vous trouve si belle,
De grâce, dites toujours non!

Oui, dans votre bouche jolie,
Mettrait l'Amour à vos genoux;
Il y voudrait passer sa vie,
Et j'en serais, je crois, jaloux!
C'est être téméraire, Adèle,
Mais mon délire est mon pardon;
Ah! quand l'Amour vous trouve belle,
De grâce aussi dites-lui non!

A yes from your lips, whispering—
Lips I adore!—sounds heaven-sent:
A zephyr borne on azure wing
Murmurs it to my heart's content.
Ah! Be it but for me, Adèle!
Pardon a slight suspicion, though:
If one thinks you a beauteous belle,
I pray you ever tell him no!

A yes from your mouth, oh so fair,
Would cast Love, worshiping, before you,
Happy to live his whole life there;
And, jealous, I would still adore you!
Yes, bold and brash am I, Adèle,
But madness earns my pardon! Oh!
If Love thinks you a lovely belle,
I pray, likewise, you tell him no!

[Louis-] Armand Garreau (1817–65)

Armand Garreau was born in Cognac, France, in 1817. As an adolescent Garreau was sent to Paris to be educated. Financial difficulties prevented him from completing his study of law, however, and he returned to Cognac, where he married Marie-Louise Dumontel, a Creole from Martinique. Attracted by the promise of wealth in the United States, Garreau took his wife and child to Louisiana in 1841. Once in New Orleans, he immediately began to teach in a private school for boys. Along with another French exile, Eugène Supervielle, Garreau established a small French weekly, *Le Démocrite*, in 1848. Although *Le Démocrite* died after only nine issues, Garreau worked for several other papers, including *La Revue louisianaise*. In 1849 Garreau's novel *Louisiana* was published in Charles Testut's *Veillées louisianaises*. The novel was overtly antislavery, and Garreau returned to France soon after it appeared.

He began another weekly in France and soon became part of a political society that included Victor Hugo. Garreau's radical republican opinions put his name on Napoléon III's list of *proscrits*. Garreau continued to write and in 1855 published four serialized novellas, two based on popular antislavery themes, *Le Nègre marron* and *Bras coupé*. After several other failed ventures, Garreau returned to New Orleans in 1858. During the Civil War he joined the Confederate Army; his son was killed at Vicksburg. Armand Garreau died in New Orleans on March 28, 1865.

A Nina

Ma Nina, mon chienchien, mon rat musqué, mon ange,
Tu souris, je le vois. Cela te semble étrange
(Toi qui n'es rien, hélas! qu'un beau petit glaçon)
De voir de quel amour imbécile je t'aime!
Et, bien sûr, tu te dis froidement à toi-même:
"Je crois décidément qu'il est fou, ce garçon."

Along with Constant Lepouzé, another French émigré, Armand Garreau was one of the white educators most respected among Creoles of color. In the obituary published in *La Tribune de la Nouvelle Orléans,* one admirer claimed that most of his community owed its instruction to Armand Garreau, who made no racial distinctions when it came to "spreading the benefits of education." Of all those who mourned the passing of the "eminent writer," he said, "none regret it more than the numerous friends that this man of true merit has made in the population of color of this city."[1]

Although we are unable to state without a doubt that "For Nina" was written by Armand Garreau, there are good reasons to believe that it was. First, "For Nina," has considerable literary merit, and by the time of his death, Garreau had become an experienced writer. He had written several novels, short stories, and some poetry. Moreover, toward the end of the 1840s, Garreau had written a humorous poem for *La Dindonade de Saint-Martinville* and signed it "A. G." Garreau's relationship to the Creole of color community makes its publication in *La Tribune* (Dec. 1865) not surprising.

---

1. Caryn Cossé Bell, *Revolution, Romanticism, and the Afro-Creole Protest Tradition in Louisiana* (Baton Rouge: Louisiana State University, 1997), 119. See also Edward Laroque Tinker, *Les Ecrits de langue française en Louisiane au 19ème siècle* (Paris: Librarie Ancienne Honoré Champion, 1932); Auguste Viatte, "Complément à la bibliographie louisianaise d'Edward Larocque Tinker," *Revue de Louisiane* 3, no. 2 (1974): 31.

For Nina

Nina! O angel, muskrat, poodle mine!
You sneer—you icicle of looks divine!—
And muse, no doubt: "How curious that the lad
Loves me with passion passing daft!" Ah, yes...
Indeed!... And, with your cold hard-heartedness,
You add: "For sure, the poor boy must be mad."

Quand, sur ton canapé, ma belle nonchalante,
Tu reposes ta main sur ma lèvre brûlante;
Quand tu baisses sur moi ton grand œil triomphant,
Et quand tes blonds cheveux traînent sur ton épaule,
O chère paresseuse, il te paraît fort drôle
De me voir à genoux pleurer comme un enfant.

Depuis l'heure où tu t'es joyeusement perdue,
Et pour cinq cents dollars bien et dûment vendue,
Je n'ai jamais senti qu'un marbre entre mes bras,
Un granit froid et dur au milieu de flamme!
C'est ton corps que j'étreins, et je voudrais ton âme!
Mais chacun par malheur sait que tu n'en as pas.

C'est bien la peine, hélas! d'avoir ce front de reine!
Cette bouche, ce nez, ces yeux!... C'est bien la peine
D'être belle à damner un saint, ô mon bijou,
Lorsque sous la peau blanche, à la fois ferme et fine,
De ton appétissante et mignonne poitrine,
Dieu, pour mon désespoir, n'a placé qu'un caillou!

O languid lovely! When you sprawl, divaned,
And on my burning lips you place your hand;
When you cast down on me your gaze unfeeling;
And when your blond locks graze your shoulder, oh!
How droll it is—as you loll, lazing, so—
To see this weeping child, by your side, kneeling.

How happily you yielded to me when
Five hundred dollars was your price! Since then,
A marble block is all my arms enfold,
Cold and hard granite midst my cravings' fire!
I hug your flesh; your soul is my desire!
And yet, you have none, if sad truth be told.

What good that regal brow, those eyes? What good
That nose, that mouth, fit for a queen? What could
All that saint-damning beauty serve—O rare,
Fair gem!—when God has placed within that white,
Sweet, tantalizing breast, for my delight,
Alas, naught but a rock, for my despair!

La Cigale et la Fourmi

Quittant le toit champêtre,
La Cigale, un été,
Dans la grande cité
En garni vint se mettre.
Son nouveau logement
Ne fut qu'un trou bien sombre,
Flanqué sinistrement
En haut d'un vieux décombre.

Là n'était nuit et jour
Que tristesse éternelle.
Aucune ritournelle,
Pas un seul chant d'amour;
Et la belle nature
Dépouillait sur le seuil,
Sa robe de verdure
Pour un manteau de deuil.

La nouvelle arrivée
Trouva qu'en sa maison
Tout manquait d'horizon.
Et, dans sa chambre nue,

Edgar Grima (1847–1939)

Edgar Grima was born in New Orleans in 1847 into an old Creole family. Educated at Jefferson Academy, Grima was a state notary and eventually became an attorney. Between 1889 and 1922, he published thirty-six poems, all but one appearing in *Comptes-rendus de L'Athénée louisianais*. "The Cricket and the Ant" and "The Wolf and the Stork" appeared there in 1899. Unlike "The Cricket and the Ant," "The Wolf and the Stork" is told in a black Creole dialect.

The Cricket and the Ant

One summer, Madame Cricket[a]
Decided to go down
And take a room in town,
Leaving her country thicket.
Her new home was a mere
Hovel, a hole: a crack
Atop the rubble, drear,
Of some dismal old shack.

There, naught but sadness: done,
All joy; by night, by day,
No cheerful roundelay,
No song of love, not one!
Now nature, late so fair,
Stripped bare before her door,
And standing, somber, there,
A cloak of mourning wore,

The new arrival found
Her digs most limited;
Her room, a naked bed.
What's more, the slightest sound,

Le moindre frôlement
De son aile fragile
Disait amèrement:
"Que viens-tu faire en ville?"

Dame Cigale avait
Une grande famille.
Les petits, ça fourmille,
Comme chacun le sait.
Pour le cœur d'une mère
Qui ne veut que leur bien,
C'est besogne légère
Que veiller sur eux bien.

Mais la dame frivole
S'ennuyait au logis,
Et malgré leurs hauts cris
Voilà qu'elle s'envole,
Entonnant follement
Un gai refrain de fête,
Fuyant éperdument
Petits et maisonnette.

Elle n'a plus qu'un soin:
Que son aile argentée,
Au soleil agitée,
L'emmène loin, bien loin,
Dans la salle brillante
Où n'entrent pas les pleurs,
Où chacun danse et chante
Et se pare de fleurs.

Elle veut dans l'ivresse
D'une folle gaîté,
Chanter sa liberté,
Oublier la tristesse;
Et dans l'entraînement
Du bonheur qui la grise,
Dépenser largement.
Qu'importe après, la bise?

Her wing's minutest flutter,
And, not without self-pity,
Bitterly she would mutter:
"Why came I to the city?"

Now, many a child had she;
For crickets, as you know,
Have kin galore, and so
Lack not for progeny.
Were she like any mother,
One thought were hers: to wit,
To mind and care for it
As much as any other.

But such is her dismay
At all she finds awry,
That, loudly though they cry,
She chirps gaily away;
Flighty, no thought in mind,
She flies off, just like that,
Happy to leave behind
Her brood and habitat.

Naught has she but one care:
That her silver-hued wing,
In the sun flittering,
Whisk her far, far, to where—
No tears!—bathed all in light,
Singing, dancing for hours
And hours, garbed all in flowers,
Life is a banquet bright.

There, in the heady bliss
Of madcap revelry,
To fete her liberty,
She would all woe dismiss;
And, swept along on laughter,
Drunk on her joy, she would
Spend wildly, all she could:
So what if winds came after?

Elle en avait assez
De son rôle de mère
Et ne songe plus guère
Aux petits délaissés,
Qui, dans le vieux décombre,
Loin des bois embaumés,
Dans leur chambrette sombre
Sont peut-être affamés.

Bientôt avec l'automne
Vint la rude saison
Qui n'a d'autre chanson
Que le cri monotone
Du grillon au foyer,
Où la bûche allumée
Se plaît à pétiller,
S'en allant en fumée.

Dame Cigale alors
Sentant frémir son aile,
Tente une ritournelle.
Mais hélas! Vains efforts!
L'aile ne sait plus battre.
Inerte sur le sol
Elle vient de s'abattre;
Plus de chant, plus de vol.

Mais, dans le vieux décombre,
Travaillant tout l'été
Quand l'autre avait chanté,
Prévoyant le jour sombre
La Fourmi pour demain,
Entassait dans ses caves,
Des petits morts de faim
Les dernières épaves.

Cette fable s'adresse à vous,
O mères de famille, époux,
Frères, que le plaisir entraîne:
Qui trop souvent, brisant la chaîne,
Oubliez le foyer sacré,

No more her thoughts awaken
To motherhood and love;
And scarcely thinks she of
Her little ones forsaken,
Who now—a-ground, a-grovel,
Far from the wood sweet-scented—
Lie in their dismal hovel,
Starving and unlamented.

Come autumn—harsh and long—
One hears one sound alone:
The chirping monotone
Of cricket's hearthside song,
As the logs, gently glowing,
Crack, crackle with delight,
And fall to embers, blowing
Their smoke into the night.

Madame, much moved, feels her
Wing give a twitch, a flutter,
Tries a refrain... Ah, but her
Efforts are vain! No whir,
No whizz, no chirp... No sound!
And, weak-winged, she falls, lying
Motionless, to the ground:
Finished, her song, her flying!

Meanwhile, back in the rubble,
Working the summer through,
While Cricket sang—as you
Recall!—foreseeing trouble,
Madame Ant took great pains
To fill her larder with
The last starving remains
Of Madame's kin and kith.

This fable is for you, O mothers
Tempted by pleasure, husbands, brothers—
All of you who, too frequently,
Breaking the bonds of family,
Neglect the sacred hearth at leisure,

Pour semer vos écus au gré
De vos goûts, de votre caprice.
Est-il bien grand le sacrifice
Que vous impose le devoir?
Non.—Rien qu'un peu de bon vouloir.

De cette fable écoutez la morale
    Toute sage vraiment
    En son enseignement:
"Ne faites pas ce que fait la Cigale."

Le Loup et la Cigogne

Michié Loup-gros-gavion li si content bafré
Qui li jamain gardé ça qui lapé mangé
Et le valé si tant gros bef avec zognon,
Qu'ain jour ain gros dézo croché dans so gavion.
Li té olé hélé mais li té pas capab.
Li commencé débat et li té per comme djab.
Alorse li prend so pate pou li fait signe Docter.
Et ça Docter la fait faut mo dit vous aster:
Docter la galopé (c'était ain vié zozo
Té té pélé Cigogne) pou halé so dézo;
Et li fouré so bec où dézo rété,
Et sauvé la vie Loup comme ain béte qui li té.
Va oir cofaire et va conain comment Docters
Qui cou traité tout moun trompé dans yé zaffaires:
Pou ca li fait, gouloupia la té bien content
Mais quand Docter Cigogne té mandé li l'argent
Pou grand service li té baye li, coquin la dit:
"Ga, couri to chimin, zozo pate longue, couri,
To capab dit merci Bon Djé to sauvé to la tête,"
Et pauv Docter Cigogne couri comme ain vié béte.

88

Blithely to go where whim and pleasure
Beckon, to sow your wealth. And all
For what? Tell me, does duty's call
Demand great sacrifice?... No, merely
That you act lovingly, sincerely.

By the wise moral of this tale, I bid
    You listen as you ought,
    And let yourself be taught:
"Pray you not do as Madame Cricket did."

------

a. Even though a *cigale* is actually a cicada, most, if not
   all, who have translated the La Fontaine subtext opt
   for "cricket." In the last two sections, the lines have
   been reformatted to reflect their syllable count,
   traditional in fables since La Fontaine. Note too that
   in the original, lines one and four in stanza three do
   not rhyme.

The Wolf and the Stork

Monsieur Wolf-Mighty-Gullet him be so
Happy him eat, him sometime never know
Just what him put in mouth!... One day, him try
Swallow big dinner—beef with onion... Ayyy!
Big bone him stick in throat! Wolf try go yell,
But no can do... Poor devil, scared like hell,
Him wave paw up, down, over... Make sign how
Him big need Doctor, and him big need now!...
Doctor run quick—him old bird So-and-So,
Old Stork him come for pull bone out... Him go
Stick beak down throat where bone stick stuck... But be
Big fool him come save Wolf!... Now you go see
How Doctor, them cure people, sure! But get
Hoodwink when come to business, you just bet!
Glutton Wolf glad big favor Stork come do,
But time him pay for cure, Wolf say: "Ha! You
Silly thing! Long-leg fool! Go! Go run way!
Thank God me let you! Him save you today!
Pay?... Me no kill you! That plenty enough!..."
Poor Doctor Stork, him stupid... Go run off.

"Henry"

When it first appeared in *La Tribune* on September 24, 1865, "The South's Constant Revolt" was signed by "Henry." "Henry" likewise contibuted several poems to *La Tribune,* including "L'Ignorance," which appeared in May 28, 1865. But the poem "Washington and Lincoln," which appeared in *La Tribune* on May 17, 1865, was signed by Henry Train, giving rise to the possibility that "Henry" was in fact Henry Train. We know little about Henry Train except that he was a white attorney who worked with Josiah Fisk. Fisk and Train advertised their law firm in *La Tribune,* leading some to suspect that Henry Train was a Creole of color, but in *My Passage at the New Orleans Tribune,* Jean-Charles Houzeau, editor of *La Tribune* from 1864 to 1868, refers to Train as a white man. Moreover, there were no "colored" lawyers before the Civil War.

The other "Henry" to whom "The South's Constant Revolt" may be attributed is Henry Rey, a Creole of color, a spiritualist, and an aspiring writer commissioned as a captain in the First Native Guards under General Butler. Indeed the historian Caryn Cossé Bell attributes an earlier appearance of the poem "L'Ignorance" to Henry Rey. It appeared in *L'Union,* September 27, 1862.

La Rebellion du Sud en Permanence

Réponse à un ami qui me demandait
si ma muse était muette.

Oui, ma muse est muette en ces jours d'épouvante;
Lorsque l'esclavagisme épanche en vain son fiel,
Lorsque du Roi Coton les dignes sycophantes,
De leurs immondes vœux importunent le ciel,
Que pourrait-elle faire et que doit-elle dire?
Sa mission d'amour, de paix, de vérité,
Lui permet-elle, ami, d'exécrer, de maudire
Ces lâches oppresseurs de toute humanité?

"The South's Constant Revolt" is a poetic response to a political catastrophe. The speaker of the poem replies to a friend "who asked me if my muse lay silent." This is a reference to elections held earlier that month wherein Democrats had won statewide. They promptly declared Louisiana a white state, abolished the 1864 constitution (which guaranteed equal rights and universal male suffrage) over the veto of the governor, and invested John T. Monroe, a leader of the white supremacist group the Southern Cross, as mayor of New Orleans. In 1866, when several hundred people from all of New Orleans' racial and linguistic communities tried to meet to reinstate the 1864 constitution, Monroe permitted the police and armed whites to prevent the assembly. The subsequent melee, known as the Massacre of 1866 or the Mechanics Hall massacre, left dozens dead.[1]

---

1. Michel Fabre, "The New Orleans Press and French-Language Literature by Creoles of Color," in *Multilingual America: Transnationalism, Ethnicity, and the Languages of American Literature*, ed. Werner Sollors (New York: New York University Press, 1998), 29–49; Caroline Senter, "Creole Poets on the Verge of a Nation," in *Creole: The History and Legacy of Louisiana's Free People of Color*, ed. Sybil Kein (Baton Rouge: Louisiana State University Press, 2000), 276–94; Caryn Cossé Bell, *Revolution, Romanticism, and the Afro-Creole Protest Tradition in Louisiana* (Baton Rouge: Louisiana State University Press, 1997), 233–40.

The South's Constant Revolt

Reply to a friend who asked me
if my muse lay silent

Yes, silent is my muse these fearsome days.
When slavery foul has spread its gall in vain,
And when King Cotton's base habitués,
In sycophantic dignity, constrain
The heavens with obscene prayer, what would she do?
What could she say? Would love, and truth, and peace—
Her goals!—have her revile those scoundrels, who
Oppress the human race without surcease?

Quand la presse est vendue à l'or de l'esclavage,
Quand le spectre du Sud sans vergogne et sans peur,
Ajoute à ses forfaits l'universel outrage
D'armer la barbarie au profit de l'erreur,
Pour combattre le Nord, dont, à ses yeux, le crime
Est d'être à tout jamais l'asile respecté
De tous les libres cœurs que l'arbitraire opprime,
Et ton sacré refuge, ô sainte liberté!

Quand le Sud réfractaire où l'horrible domine;
Condamné par le ciel, la raison, le devoir,
Vaincu, déshonoré, dans sa lutte intestine
Pour son indépendance et le cruel pouvoir
D'étendre l'esclavage et de river les chaînes
De frères, comme tous, fils d'un Père éternel,
Doués, comme les blancs, de facultés humaines,
Et comme eux animés du rayon immortel;

Quand ce Sud, qui portait sur sa cotte de maille:
"Esclavage des noirs et licence pour nous!"
N'est pas plus tôt vaincu sur le champ de bataille,
Qu'il essaie au scrutin, de son pouvoir jaloux,
D'annuler, par le dol, ce que la Providence,
Par arrêt du canon, a déjà décrété:
Rivons les fers, dit-il, par rebelle ordonnance,
Et torturons les noirs suspects de loyauté.

Voilà pourquoi ma muse est muette et violée,
Car elle pressent bien plus d'un nouveau combat,
Et l'espérance, ami, de son sein envolée,
La laisse morne et triste, et son destin l'abat.
Quoi qu'on fasse, mon luth ne peut vibrer de rage,
Il prêche la concorde et la fraternité;
Aux opprimés il dit: Frères, debout, courage,
L'heure est près de sonner, sauvez la liberté!

When slavery's venal gold has bought the press;
When the South's wanton specter, holding forth,
Would, to its evils, add the sinfulness
Of arming savagery against the North;
That land whose only crime is to have been
Ever a refuge where free hearts might be
Safe from oppression; haven sure, wherein
You live secure, O blessèd liberty!

When the rebellious South, horror's domain,
Condemned by reason, duty, heaven; disgraced,
Dishonored in its treasonous campaign
To flout our nationhood; destined to taste
Defeat in its dread aim, basely avowed,
To sow slavery's woes, enchain those who—
Our brothers, sons of God—no less endowed
Than whites with souls and minds, are human too;

When that South—with these words emblazoning
Its coat of mail: "For the blacks, slavery!
For us, free rein!"—was, by war's reckoning,
No sooner crushed, than, by foul infamy
It would re-forge the chains, and, at the polls,
Subvert the cannon's will, for Providence
Decreed; then, lo! it said: "Let those black souls
Suffer for their un-Southern sentiments!"

This, friend, is why my ravaged muse lies still;
For she can sense now many a struggle brewing.
All hope, fled from her breast, undone her will,
Sad is she that fell fate vowed her undoing.
Ah, no! My lute, though she would try her best,
Cannot sing rage: she preaches harmony.
"Brothers, stand tall," she tells the sore oppressed.
"Soon tolls the hour: keep safe your liberty!"

Armand Lanusse (1812–67)

Armand Lanusse's role in the history of Louisiana's Creoles of color cannot be overstated. Born in New Orleans in 1812, Lanusse was educated in Paris at the prestigious Ecole Polytechnique. Early on Lanusse sought to publicize the myriad contributions Creoles of color had made to the intellectual and cultural life of New Orleans. Lanusse played a leading role in the creation of a literary journal that featured the work of Creoles of color. The *Album littéraire: journal des jeunes gens, amateurs de littérature* appeared in 1843 and published work by both Creoles, such as Terrance Rouquette, and Creoles of color. Lanusse produced no more than six issues of the *Album,* which was bold for its time and place. In it he published "Un Mariage de conscience," a story that sharply criticizes *plaçage,* the practice whereby a (typically fair-skinned and beautiful) young Creole woman of color would be "placed" with—that is, become the concubine of—a rich white man in exchange for a large sum of money, property, and future support. But Armand

Epigramme

"Vous ne voulez donc pas renoncer à Satan,"
Disait un bon pasteur à certaine bigote
Qui d'assez gros péchés, à chaque nouvel an,
Venait lui présenter l'interminable note.
"Je veux y renoncer," dit-elle, "pour jamais;
Mais avant que la grâce en mon âme scintille,
Pour m'ôter tout motif de pécher désormais,
Que ne puis-je, pasteur—Quoi donc?—*placer* ma fille?"

Le Carnaval[a]

L'hiver, sémillante Palmyre,
Reprend, hélas! son triste cours.
Décembre, les vents, tout conspire
Pour effaroucher les amours.
En les ralliant, la Folie

Lanusse may be best remembered as the editor of the first anthology of African American literature, *Les Cenelles: choix de poésies indigènes,* which was published in 1845.

In an equally important undertaking, Lanusse helped persuade the city of New Orleans to permit the completion of a Catholic school for indigent orphans of color. In 1832 Madame Bernard Couvent, a pious woman and former slave of African origins, had left the city money to construct and operate such a school, but local opposition to the project delayed construction for a dozen years. Armand Lanusse and the Reverend Manehault overcame the opposition, and the school was completed in 1848. Armand Lanusse became its headmaster in 1852 and remained in that position until his death in 1867.

"Epigram," a stinging critique of *plaçage,* and "Mardi Gras" were published in *Les Cenelles* in 1845.

Epigram

"Madame will not renounce the Devil," said
A pastor to a zealous pietist,
Who, every New Year, brought her sins, outspread
Before him in a never-ending list.
"I would," said she, "indeed renounce him. But,
Before grace sparks my soul, tell me I can...
To rid all need for future sinning..." "What?..."
"Set up my daughter with a rich white man!"

Mardi Gras

Drear winter—sprightly, pert Palmyre—
Returns, alas! The winds thereof
Plot with December's storms, I fear,
To frighten off all who would love.
But Folly rallies them once more

Donne partout l'heureux signal!—
Bannissons la mélancolie;
Voici le temps du Carnaval.

Dans cette foule où l'on se presse,
Déjà j'entends autour de toi,
Mille amans répéter sans cesse:
"Je t'aime… Palmyre, aime moi!—"
Sans craindre d'être inconséquente,
Dis à tous ce refrain banal:
"Je vous aime et serai constante."
Tout est permis en Carnaval.

Mais lorsque ta bouche rieuse
Leur promet amour éternel,
Songe qu'à moi, belle oublieuse,
Tu fis un aveu plus formel.
Pour mieux lier notre existence
Je veux qu'un serment conjugal
Ait pour nous plus de consistance
Qu'une promesse en Carnaval.

––––––––––

a. "Le Carnaval" was set to the tune of
    "Les Oiseaux que l'hiver exile."

And sounds the happy call: Huzza!
Away with melancholy, for
Now is the time of Mardi Gras!

Pressing close in this milling throng,
A thousand lovers crowd about you.
Already I hear, all day long:
"Palmyre... I cannot live without you!..."
With no fear of frivolity,
Sing each this bland rejoinder: "Ah!
I love you, and shall faithful be!"
All's fair in love and Mardi Gras!

But as your laughing lips foretell
Eternal love to each and all,
Think of me, my forgetful belle,
And your more serious vow recall.
So may we swear and solemnize
A wedding vow—proper, bourgeois—
To join us in more solid wise
Than promises at Mardi Gras.

Mosaïque[a]

A une Amie

Plus fraîche que la fleur que voit naître l'aurore,
Au milieu du printemps qui l'embellit encore;
A l'éclat unissant le parfum le plus doux,
La ravissante Estelle apparaît parmi nous...

 —F. Calongne

Elevée au milieu du désert de la vie,
La fleur modeste et pure et que le monde oublie
Mérite bien souvent nos soins les plus touchants.
Insensible aux regards, l'aimable violette
Ne se montre jamais, et chérit sa retraite:
Ainsi que toi, doux ange, elle suit ses penchants.
Tu puisais tes attraits, charmante créature,

Alexandre Latil (1816–51)

Alexandre Latil's family had its origins in the colonial period. Latil was born in New Orleans in 1816 and educated at the best schools there. He was diagnosed with leprosy while still an adolescent, and he suffered from the disease all his adult life. Before learning of his illness, Latil had been engaged to marry, and when he offered to break the engagement, the young woman refused. Latil's family arranged to move him to a small cabin in Bayou Saint-Jean, where land had been set aside for lepers. Latil then married his faithful fiancée so that she could accompany him there. Some of Latil's poetry was published in the *Gazette de Bâton Rouge* in 1840. In 1841 he published a volume of poetry, *Les Ephémères*. The work is inspired by the French romantics, and although some poems express a profound sense of loss and despair, others, such as "Mosaic," "For Mademoiselle Adèle," and "For Madame C * * *," celebrate the joy and beauty of youth, however brief. Latil died of his disease in 1851. Alexandre Latil and his wife, whose name we do not know, were remembered in Charles Testut's affectionate tributes "For Monsieur Alex. Latil" and "On the Death of the Author of *Les Ephémères*," both included in this volume.

Mosaic

> Fresher yet than the fair bloom of the morn,
> Amidst the springtime of the year newborn,
> Joining dawn's splendor with the scent of spring,
> Estelle appears among us, ravishing...
>
> —F. Calongne[a]

For a Lady Friend

Often, that flower of life's desert recesses
Is worthiest of our dearest tendernesses:
Chaste, timid flower that life and world forget.
Unseen by human glance, content, it dwells
In solitude, to do as nature tells.
Sweet angel, you are as that violet.
From your heart's crucible that, full, distills

Au creuset de ton cœur, où la vertu s'épure.
Bien heureux le mortel à qui le ciel, un jour,
Accordera ce cœur, et qui de l'hyménée
Recevant ce trésor, ô vierge fortunée!
Y saura faire naître un éternel amour!

    5 mai 1839

----

a. Latil numbered each poem in the collection. "Mosaique"
    is éphémère 7.

A Mlle Adèle * * *a

O fille du printemps douce et touchante image
        D'un cœur modeste et vertueux,
Du sein de ce gazon tu remplis ce bocage
        De ton parfum délicieux.

    —Mme d'Hautpoul

On dit que la charmante Adèle
Possède grâces et douceur.
Que l'on serait heureux près d'elle,
Si l'on pouvait toucher son cœur!
Mais pour parvenir à lui plaire,
Il faut égaler ses vertus;
Et tous mes soins seraient perdus,
Si j'entreprenais de le faire.

De la rose qui vient d'éclore
Elle a l'éclat et la fraîcheur;
Mais plus simple, elle joint encore
La modestie à la candeur.
Je sais que ma muse légère
Est peu digne de ses appas,
Et les chanter ne pourrait pas,
Quand elle essaîrait de le faire.

Your virtue, you drew that great charm that fills
Your being; happy the man whom generous heaven
Will grant that heart in wedded joy possessed—
That treasure, O fair virgin, fortune-blessed—
Whence love, pure and eternal, shall be given!

May 5, 1839

----

a. Adolphe Fauconné de Calongne (1836–89) was both
   Alexandre Latil's first cousin and a poet, but since this
   poem was composed in 1839, only three years after
   Adolphe Calongne's birth, these lines cannot be attributed
   to him. Viatte argues that they may have been penned by
   Calongne's older brother.

For Mlle Adèle * * *

> O child of spring—sweet image of a heart
>   In modesty and virtue spent—
> You fill the woodland bosom's every part
>   With your perfume's fair, fragrant scent.
>
> —Mme d'Hautpoul[a]

With charm and grace they say Adèle
Is blessed, and well-possessed thereof.
What a joy, by her side to dwell,
Could one but touch her heart with love!
But one must have such virtues too
If one would hope to gladden her;
Thus all my efforts wasted were,
To do so, if I chose to do.

Of the new, freshly blooming rose
She has the pure, bright radiance;
And simpler still, that guileless pose
Of chaste and artless elegance.
My muse, alas, too weak thereto,
Is most unworthy, I confess,
To sing praise to her comeliness,
Were it to venture so to do.

Si quelquefois la perfidie
Se pare d'attraits séduisants,
Je le dirai, sans flatterie,
Adèle ignore ces instants.
Ah! Pardonnez au téméraire
Qui vient de tracer ce portrait:
Un Béranger seul le pourrait,
S'il entreprenait de le faire.

1836

---

a. "A Mlle Adèle" is éphémère 9.

Sur la Mort de H. Boussuge[a]

Oui, la vie est un songe et la mort un réveil.

—Arnault

Va, tu n'es pas à plaindre, ô toi dont l'existence
Fut si belle et si calme au sein de la souffrance!
Ton âme s'exhala comme un dernier adieu,
Doucement résignée aux volontés de Dieu.
Ah! ne regrette pas un monde injuste, impie:
Pour un séjour divin, une éternelle vie,
Tu ne laisses qu'un lieu d'ineffables douleurs,
Séjour affreux de deuil, de chagrins et de pleurs!
Boussuge, le destin qui, loin de ta patrie,
T'arrache à l'amitié d'une mère chérie,
Et brise à son aurore un si bel avenir,
Te laisse dans nos cœurs un touchant souvenir.

août 1839

---

a. "Sur la Mort de H. Boussuge" is éphémère 10.

If, at times, faithless treachery
One hides behind charm's fair disguise,
I say—meaning no flattery!—
Adèle behaves in no such wise.
Ah! Pardon, pray, the rash one who
Dares limn the portrait here begun:
Béranger is the only one
To do so, if he chose to do.

1836

---

a. Mme d'Hautpoul was a French writer (b. 1763).

On the Death of H. Boussuge[a]

Yes, life is but a dream, and death, a waking.

—Arnault[b]

No! We need not mourn for your life, a thing
Of tranquil beauty midst your suffering!
Calmly resigned to God's will, like a breath,
A last farewell, your soul whispered your death.
Grieve not the loss of a world foul and fell:
You quit a place of woes too dire to tell—
Of tears, Boussuge, and miseries malign—
To dwell, eternal, in a home divine.
The fate that strips you of your fatherland,
That rips you from a cherished mother and
Shatters, at dawn, your glorious destiny,
Leaves in our hearts your tender memory.

August 1839

---

a. Hans Boussuge founded the semiweekly journal *La Créole.*
Established in 1837, *La Créole* was published in New Orleans.
b. Antoine Arnault (1766–1834), best remembered as the author
of eight books of fables, was also a dramatist and wrote an
important biography of Napoléon.

A Corinne * * *[a]

Un amour malheureux est un bonheur encore.

—Mme Desbordes-Valmore

Il faut te fuir, séduisante Corinne:
Il faut te fuir et ne plus te revoir:
De tes attraits la puissance divine
Troubla mon être, et dicta ce devoir.

J'ai vu tes yeux où la candeur respire,
Tes traits charmants, ton sourire enchanteur;
Ta douce voix a causé mon délire,
Et, désormais, le tourment de mon cœur.

Oui, c'en est fait, ton image chérie
A pour jamais pris place dans mon cœur;
Pour l'effacer, il faut m'ôter la vie,
Qui n'est pour moi qu'une lente douleur.

Félicité, fantôme imaginaire,
Qu'en vain mon cœur essaya de saisir!
Ah! ne sois plus une vaine chimère
Qui se complaise à me faire souffrir.

Ne plus te voir!... qui pourrait y souscrire?
Ne plus t'entendre! oh! ce serait affreux.
Je puis t'aimer, sans jamais te le dire,
Ah! je le sens, c'est encore être heureux.

février 1839

---

a. "A Corinne" is éphémère 12.

104

For Corinne * * *

> Unhappy love is happiness no less.
>
> —Mme Desbordes-Valmore[a]

Flee you I must, bewitching belle, Corinne:
Flee you I must, nor look on you again;
The powers of your divine allure chagrin
And harry me, and thus my flight ordain.

I saw your glance, fragrant with innocence,
Your face that charmed—enchanted!—when you smiled;
And your soft voice it is that yet torments
My heart, drives mad my senses, sore beguiled.

Yes, your dear image, my belovèd friend,
Graven within my heart shall ever be;
To wipe it clean, my very life must end,
Which is naught but a long-drawn woe for me.

Joy! Phantom of the mind! How my heart tried
To seize you! But alas, it sought in vain.
Ah! Be not that chimera that takes pride
And pleasure thus to cause my grievous pain.

No more to see you!... Who could bear that lot?
No more to hear you!... Oh, the cruel duress!
Still can I love you, though I tell you not;
And merely loving you is happiness.

February 1839

---

a. Marceline Desbordes-Valmore (1786–1859) was a French poet
   whose collections include *Elégies, Marie et Romance* (1819), and
   Elégies et poésies nouvelles (1825).

A Madame C * * *[a]

(Improvisation)

...mes seuls trésors: des vers!

—Hégésippe Moreau

Le jour de votre fête est un jour bien heureux;
Tous vos amis voudraient vous adresser leurs vœux!
C'est à qui cherchera le moyen de vous plaire;
Je le voudrais aussi, mais je ne puis le faire;
Je ne puis vous offrir de présent ni de fleur;
Je n'ai que des soucis qu'arrose le malheur.
Je ne les donne point, ils ne font point envie,
Vous en cueillez assez dans le cours de la vie !
Mais recevez les vœux que fait pour vous mon cœur:
Joie et santé parfaite, image du bonheur.
Puissé-je, dans vingt ans, à ma dernière aurore,
Improviser des vers, et vous les dire encore!

1836

---

a. "A Madame C * * *" is éphémère 14.

106

For Madame C* * *

(Improvisation)

. . . My only wealth: my verse!

—Hégésippe Moreau[a]

On this, your birthday—happy day indeed!—
Your friends bestow good wishes and godspeed,
And vie with one another so to do!
Would I might, likewise, fete and honor you.
I can no flower-present offer though:
No flower but bleeding-heart have I, that woe
Waters with drops of sorrow and of strife.
I give it not; you have no need: in life
You shall pick many! But I give no less
My heartfelt wish for joy, health, happiness.
In twenty years, may I brief verses pen—
At my last dawn—and wish you so again!

1836

---

a. Hégésippe Moreau (1810–38), French writer and founder of the
satirical journal *Diogène,* is best known for his five prose tales
collected in *Myosotis* (1851).

Vers sur l'Album de Monsieur * * *: Le Forgeron

SONNET

Mon gros soufflet ventru repose dans ses plis.
Le fonçoir à la main, le coude sur l'enclume,
J'attends, gai travailleur, que mon feu se rallume:
Souffleur, viens ranimer ses rayons affaiblis.

Vous, mes chers vêtements enfumés et salis,
Sans cesse retrempés dans le brasier qui fume,
Certes, vous valez ceux que l'on dore et parfume
Pour femmes aux doux yeux, au front blancheur de lis.

Mon gros soufflet ventru, c'est vous, ma foi si vive,
Qui soufflez le foyer de mon âme plaintive,
Les habits sont mes vers que le ciel m'a donnés.

Monsieur, dans votre album où tant de gens bien nés
Sans doute on fait assaut de bon ton et de grâce,
Au forgeron obscur feriez-vous une place?

16 mai 1840

Eugène Le Blanc (1817-?)

Eugène Le Blanc, born in New Orleans in 1817, was a teacher and lover of poetry. Between 1840 and 1841 several of his poems were published in *L'Abeille* and *Courrier de la Louisiane*. A volume of Le Blanc's poetry, *Essais poétiques,* was published in Paris in 1842. "Lines in the Album of Monsieur * * *" first appeared in *Essais poétiques.*

Lines in the Album of Monsieur * * *:
The Blacksmith

SONNET

Pot-bellied bellows mine, stout, pleated lies.
Hammer in hand, elbow on anvil, I
Stand, joyous, waiting till my flame flares high:
Bellows-boy, come! Breathe life before it dies.

You, dirty, smoke-grimed clothes! Ah! How I prize
You more—boiled clean, soaked and soaked, by and by!—
Than those—perfumed, gilt-sewn—that gratify
Lily-browed ladies' gaze, in fancy's guise.

My keen faith: you, pot-bellied bellows stout,
Breath of my plaintive soul, now in, now out;
Those clothes: these verses mine, by heaven bestowed.

Friend, in your album, where men *à la mode*
Have fought to pen their names with stylish grace,
Can this mere blacksmith hope to find a place?

May 16, 1840

Au Père Chocarne

Mon Très Révérend Père,
Un nègre obscur et méprisé,
Ecoutait enivré, la semaine dernière,
Votre verbe irisé.

Il sentait dans son être,
Entrer comme un éclair de *foi:*
Il allait rejeter son consolant "Peut-être"
Et rembrasser la croix;

Mais cet homme, ce nègre, ô Révérend Père,
Tandis qu'il se laissait emporter, éperdu,
Au tumulte pompeux de votre accent austère,
Détacha ses regards et son cœur de la chaire,
Et le suprême appel qu'il avait entendu,
Comme un soupir divin, adresser à son âme,
Ne fut bientôt qu'une mourante flamme,
Qu'un fugitif souvenir
Que la réalité fit vite évanouir;
Car il se rappela que, même dans cette église,
Les apôtres du Christ souffrent que l'on méprise
Que l'on relègue, en certains bancs,
Non pas de grands pécheurs, non pas d'impurs tyrans,
Mais bien de pauvres gens
Dont le seul tort, dont le seul crime,
Est d'avoir
Le teint noir.

"Pierre l'Hermite"

"Pierre l'Hermite" is a pseudonym for an author whose identity remains a mystery. "To Père Chocarne" was published in *La Tribune* on April 16, 1867.

To Père Chocarne

Last week, O most Révérend Père,
A black—poor nobody!—was listening,
At mass, impassioned, to your sermon's prayer,
    With glory glistening.

He felt, despite his soul's long lapse,
    A flash of faith streak through him then;
And, casting off his comforting "Perhaps,"
    Would clutch the cross again.

But when, O Reverend Father, he—this black—
Swept along by your words' tumultuous flow,
Turned his heart from the pulpit, glancing back,
He learned that heaven's majestic call (ah, woe!),
Though first a sigh unto his soul, became—
    And oh, how soon!—a dying flame,
        A fleeting memory
Fading before a harsh reality.
    For even here he realized
That shame prevails: here in Christ's temple, whose
Apostles suffer some to be despised
And sent, in scorn, to sit in separate pews;
Not sinners vile, nor tyrants of the yoke,
    But simply poor and wretched folk
        Whose only sin
        Is their black skin.

Vous allez donc tonner contre cette injustice:
Du temple Jésus-Christ sut chasser les marchands,
    A votre tour, chassez-en les méchants,
    Et ne paraissez pas en être complice.
En pensant au poète obscur et méprisé
    Que captiva votre verbe irisé,
    Vous leur direz ô très Révérend Père,
Qu'un blanc, qui ne veut pas qu'un nègre soit son frère,
N'a plus le droit sacré d'appeler Dieu son père.

In thunderous tones you must this wrong condemn!
Just as Christ cast the money-lenders out,
   So too must you the miscreants rout
Lest you appear to be in league with them.
Remember, thus, this poet-nobody—
Poet scorned, but enraptured, listening
   To your prayer, glory-glistening.
O Révérend Père, tell them that the white
Himself it is who sins in heaven's sight:
He who denies black men as brothers would
Deny, too, God the Father's fatherhood.

A un Ami Qui M'Accusait de Plagiat[a]

Quoi, mon ami doute de toi, ma muse,
Ah! viens t'unir encore à mon ardeur
Pour lui prouver que jamais à la ruse
Je ne voudrais devoir le nom d'auteur.
A mériter ce nom je ne m'applique,
Il est bien vrai, je le dis sur ma foi;
Mais seulement ici je revendique
Quelques couplets qui sont vraiment de moi.

St. Léon, quoi, toi dont l'âme est si bonne,
Tu viens me dire avec un air malin,
Que ces couplets sont d'une autre personne
Et que j'ai fait un indigne larcin.
Pour me railler en vain ta voix rustique
Du dieu des vers invoquera la loi.
Mais revenons, ici, je revendique
Quelques couplets qui sont vraiment de moi.

Mirtil-Ferdinand Liotau

(ca. 1800–1847)

Mirtil-Ferdinand Liotau, a Creole of color, was born in New Orleans, probably in the first decade of the nineteenth century. Liotau contributed one poem to the *Album littéraire;* "An Impression" was published in 1843. In 1845 eight of Liotau's poems were published in *Les Cenelles.* The poems included here come from *Les Cenelles* and range in tone from the earnest piety of "For Ida" and "An Impression" to the playful and humorous "My Old Hat" and "For a Friend Who Accused Me of Plagiarism." In fact, "For a Friend" provoked a literary duel between Liotau and Léon Sindos, another Creole of color, that took place in the pages of the newspaper *La Réforme* in April 1846. Liotau's weapon of choice was satirical acrostics. He died in New Orleans in 1847.

For a Friend Who Accused Me of Plagiarism

What? My friend doubts you, muse of mine? Ah, so!
I pray you come again and join with me
To prove to him that I would never owe
The poet's name to ruse and quackery.
I bend no effort to deserve that name,
And on my faith and honor be it known;
But here and now I merely lay my claim
To a few lines that are, indeed, my own.

Dear Saint-Léon! O noble soul and fine!
You tell me with that sly, mischievous air
That these, my verses, are not really mine,
And that I'm guilty of a foul affair!
In vain you chide and cover me with shame,
Citing Apollo's laws in rustic tone;
Once more I say: here, now, I lay my claim
To a few lines that are, indeed, my own.

Il est passé, St. Léon, ce bel âge
Où tu faisais notre admiration.
Avec ce temps a fui ton doux langage;
Tu n'as gardé que ta présomption.
De ranimer ton ardeur poétique
St. Léon cesse, elle est morte chez toi.
Mais revenons, ici, je revendique
Quelques couplets qui sont vraiment de moi.

---

a. This poem was set to the air "Amis, voici la riante
semaine."

Une Impression

Eglise Saint-Louis, vieux temple, reliquaire,
Te voilà maintenant désert et solitaire!
Ceux qui furent commis ici bas à tes soins,
Du tabernacle saint méprisant les besoins,
Ailleurs ont entraîné la phalange chrétienne.
Jusqu'à ce que chacun de son erreur revienne,
Sur tes dalles, hélas! on ne verra donc plus
S'agenouiller encor les enfants de Jésus,
Qui, l'oreille attentive et l'âme timorée,
Savouraient d'un pasteur la parole sacrée?
Et de ton sanctuaire, espace précieux,
L'encens n'enverra plus son parfum vers les cieux!—
Tes splendides autels, tes images antiques,
Tes croix, tes ornemens et tes saintes reliques,
Hélas! vont donc rester dans un profond oubli
Qui les range déjà sous son immense pli!—
O toi, temple divin, toi dernière demeure
Des hommes bien aimés que le peuple encor pleure,
Et qui, peut-être aussi, ressentant tous tes maux,
Gémissent comme nous du fond de leurs tombeaux,
Toi qui me vis enfant en ton enceinte même
Recevoir sur mon front les signes du baptême;
Hélas! ai-je grandi pour te voir en ce jour
Désert, abandonné peut-être sans retour?—
Auguste et pur asile où toute âme est ravie
Lorsque se chante en chœur la sainte liturgie,
Resteras-tu toujours privé de tout honneur?

Past, Saint-Léon, is that fair age when you
Were much admired; and now, alas, far less:
Time makes your golden language bid adieu,
And leaves you only your presumptuousness.
Cease trying to relight your talent's flame,
And, Saint-Léon, leave what is dead alone!
Once more I say: here, now, I lay my claim
To a few lines that are, indeed, my own.

An Impression

Saint Louis! Old temple, shrine!... Now, how forsaken
You stand! For those who once had undertaken
Ever to care for you, and had assured
The holy tabernacle, have abjured
And, elsewhere, led the Christian host, *en masse*.
What? Till each mends his errant ways, alas!
Shall Jesus' children nevermore be found
Kneeling in prayer upon your blessèd ground,
Or by the pastor's holy message stirred,
Each soul a-tremble on his every word?
What? No more shall the scents of incense rise
Up from your sacred precincts to the skies?...
Your splendid altars, relics, ornaments,
Rich crosses, ancient canvases, must hence
Repose, lost, in a dark oblivion
That blankets them already, every one?...
O you, temple divine, where dwelt the last
Remains of those still loved, although long past
Their days; whom yet the people mourn, and who
Feeling our woes no less than now we do,
Aghast, moan in the tomb their deep despair;
You, who it was that saw my young brow bear
Baptism's grace, there in your breast! Ah me!
Have I lived to this day only to see
You thus abandoned with no hope whatever
That you might yet renew your life? What? Never?...
Refuge august and pure, where ecstasy

Puisque jamais en vain nous prions le Seigneur,
Chrétiens, unissons-nous; quand ce Dieu tutélaire
A versé tout son sang pour nous sur le Calvaire,
Espérons qu'en ce jour lui seul puissant et fort,
En le priant du cœur changera notre sort;
Prions si nous voulons que sa miséricorde
Détruise parmi nous la haine et la discorde.
Déjà cette espérance, en tarissant nos pleurs,
N'a-t-elle point versé son baume dans nos cœurs?
N'avons-nous point revu la foule orléanaise
Quand vint la noble fête, au vieux temple tout aise?
Alors le vrai bonheur brillait dans tous les yeux,
Car tout fut oublié dans cet instant heureux!
Chrétiens, un autre effort penchera la balance
Sans doute vers la paix, gardons-en l'assurance;
Et nous verrons encor comme dans le passé,
Le peuple chaque jour au temple délaissé!

Mon Vieux Chapeau[a]

On dit que mon chapeau
Remonte au temps d'Hérode,
Qu'il n'est plus à la mode,
Qu'il m'en faut un nouveau.
Mais tout bas je répète
Que chacun a son goût;
Quand je l'ai sur la tête,
Je suis bien vu partout.

Lorsque sur un côté
Je l'ajuste avec grâce,
Chacun me donne place,
Je marche avec fierté.
Ma belle, la première,
Me dit que je suis beau,
Quand de cette manière
Je mets mon vieux chapeau.

Fills the soul as the holy liturgy
Is chanted in a blissful unison:
Tell me, must you forever stand undone,
Honor-bereft, so ever to remain?
O Christians! Naught we ask the Lord in vain:
Let us, before our God magnanimous,
Unite, and pray to Him, who shed for us
His blood on Calvary, that He, today,
Omnipotent, hear us, and sweep away,
With His most tender mercy, all the hate
And discord that can sunder, separate
Our ranks! Have we not seen such hope impart
A soothing balm unto our weeping heart?
Did we not see New Orleans throng to fete
The "noble feast" in this shrine's walls, well met
In happiness, shining from every eye,
All ills forgot?... O Christians, if we try
Again, will we not turn the tide, at last,
Toward peace, and see, as in the glorious past,
The people, faithful, flocking as before
To this deserted church, alive once more!

My Old Hat

They tell me that my hat
Goes back to Herod's day;
The style has changed, they say.
I give them tit for tat:
I need no new *chapeau;*
Taste is taste: this is mine,
And I know I look fine
No matter where I go.

When, with a touch of class,
And with a strutting stride,
I tilt it to the side,
Everyone lets me pass.
And, most of all, my belle—
When I wear it like that—
Says I'm a beau, a swell,
Dressed up in my old hat.

Ah! si dans sa bonté
Dieu me faisait la grâce
De prolonger ma race,
Que je serais flatté
De voir avant que j'aille
Dans un monde nouveau,
Un garçon de ma taille
Mettre mon vieux chapeau.

----

a. "Mon vieux chapeau" was set
   to the tune of "C'est l'eau qui
   nous fait boire."

A Ida

Ce qui me plaît en toi, ce que j'admire et j'aime,
Ce ne sont pas, Ida, tes seize ans, ta fraîcheur.
Ce n'est pas ton œil noir qui d'un amour extrême
      A su remplir mon cœur.

Ce ne sont pas non plus tes longs cheveux d'ébène,
Ni même ton corps souple aux gracieux contours;
Ni tes pieds si mignons, ni ton maintien de reine
      Ni tes riches atours.

Mais c'est cette vertu qui s'oppose sans crainte
Aux volontés d'un cœur impudique et vénal,
Cette douce candeur, cette innocence empreinte
      Sur ton front virginal.

C'est ce pur sentiment que ton âme angélique
Puise du sein d'un Dieu qui t'a donné la foi:
C'est cet accent divin de ta voix poétique
      Pour défendre sa loi.

Oui, ce sont ces attraits, Ida, je te le jure,
Qui ravissent mon cœur et m'inspirent ces chants;
Que l'écho qui vers toi les porte, vierge pure,
      Les redise longtemps!

If, in God's goodness, He
Were graciously inclined
To propagate my kind,
How flattered I would be—
As I embarked upon
Another life—thereat
To see my like put on,
Once again, my old hat.

For Ida

It is not, Ida, your dear youth that thrills
My love—your sixteen years—nor is your glowing
Glance, dark of eye, what conquered me, and fills
  My heart to overflowing.

It is not your long ebony-black tresses,
Your queen-like bearing, that my eyes admire,
Nor your form's supple-contoured sweet recesses,
  Dainty feet, rich attire.

Rather it is that heart, with virtue blessed,
That to shame's base commands will never bow;
That gentle, simple innocence impressed
  Upon your virgin brow.

It is your faith, that angel's purity
That your soul from God's very bosom draws.
It is your voice's heavenly poetry
  Commending us His laws.

Yes, Ida, by your charms inspired, I sing
The ecstasy that my heart feels therefor:
Virgin pure, may my verses, echoing,
  Praise you forevermore!

Le Melon

"Souvent notre méchanceté
N'est, tout bien compté,
Qu'une erreur grossière."
Démontrons cette vérité:
Un créole avait une melonière
Si belle et riche en fruits, que messieurs ses cochons
N'étaient nourris que de melons.
En faisant un matin sa tournée ordinaire,
Il remarqua par terre
Quelques morceaux d'écorce et des traces de pas.
Le voilà dans tous ses états,

Joseph-Auguste-André Maltrait

(1865–1937)

Joseph-Auguste-André Maltrait was born in Brittany, France, in 1865. He served as curé in Lafayette, Louisiana, from 1896 to 1908 and then in the neighboring town of Kaplan until 1921, when he retired. He returned to France and died in Saint-Lunaire, Brittany, in 1937. Maltrait contributed to the pages of *Comptes-rendus de l'Athénée louisianais* with fables such as "The Melon," first published in January 1899. It was included in the St. Martin and Voorhies anthology *Ecrits louisianais du dix-neuvième siècle* and Norman Shapiro's collection *The Fabulists French*. In their introduction St. Martin and Voorhies observe that the racial theme of "The Melon" makes it an authentically local tale.

In all probability Maltrait is also "Joseph Le Beuzit," the author of "The Preacher's Hat," which appeared in *Comptes-rendus* in March 1900. Norman Shapiro offers two reasons for this conjecture: both Maltrait and "Le Beuzit" were careless about syllable count in their compositions, and "Le Beuzit" was Maltrait's mother's maiden name. It is possible that, being a priest, Maltrait did not want his name to appear on the mildly irreverent poem "The Preacher's Hat."

The Melon

The proverb tells us that "our sin
Is often blunder in disguise."
There is, I fear, much truth therein,
As this, our fable, testifies.
A Creole had a melon patch, wherein
So many a melon grew, in such great store,
That monsieur's swine—a fancy lot, indeed—
For all their feed
Feasted on melons, nothing more.
Now, one day, as he makes his morning round,
Monsieur looks down and, scattered on the ground,

Qui s'écrie: "Il faut qu'il périsse,
Le criminel qui vient, au mépris de la loi,
Me faire l'injustice
D'entrer la nuit chez moi
Pour gaspiller mon bien!" Alors, suivant l'usage,
Il soupçonna quelqu'un du voisinage:
"C'est ce nègre et ses négrillons,"
Dit-il, "qui mangent mes melons!"
Et n'écoutant que sa colère
Il court de céans chez l'apothicaire
Acheter du poison;
(C'était, je crois, de la strichnine,)
Dont il pique un melon
De fort belle mine.
Puis, il se retire en disant:
"Mon gourmand de noiraud peut venir à présent:
Je lui promets la plus belle colique."
Le voleur vint. Sur lui, le poison fut très fort;
Le faiseur de melons au jour le trouva mort.
C'était son fils unique!

Le Chapeau du Prêcheur

Un jour, dans sa chapelle,
Un pauvre prédicant
Fit au peuple fidèle
Un discours éloquent.
Son exorde soigné fut noble et plein de charmes;
Il fit, dans ses trois points, honneur à la raison;
Vers la péroraison,
De tous les yeux ruisselèrent des larmes.
A ce spectacle inattendu,
L'orateur attendri pleure aussi, mais de joie.
De la chaire enfin descendu,
Il ajoute, en séchant un pauvre œil qui se noie:
"Mes frères, j'ai prêché trois quarts d'heure! il est temps
De passer la quête dans les bancs:
L'ouvrier, dit Saint Paul, est digne d'un salaire.
J'ai travaillé pour votre âme; j'espère
Que tous, avec amour,
En ce grand jour de fête,

He sees some bits of rind,
    And someone's tracks—before, behind,
        And all about.
"Foul criminal!" our Creole lashes out.
    "Of all the vilest ignominies!...
What? Plunder me by night?... I'll see him hang!
For sure, it's that old nigger and his gang
        Of pickaninnies!"
(So he suspected, as was customary.)
        Then, furious, off he goes
    Straightway to the apothecary
To buy some poison—strychnine, I suppose...
    He picks a melon, firm and fat,
    And pricks it full. "Well now, that's that!
My darky can come eat his fill!" he crows.
"He'll have himself a proper bellyache,
    My melon thief, make no mistake!"
The felon came. When all was said and done,
Next day, no sooner did monsieur awake
Than there... He finds him dead... His only son!

The Preacher's Hat

    A creature of the frock—
    Good preacher indigent—
    One day regaled his flock
    With sermon eloquent.
Three points—as reason dictates—it presented;
Charming and nobly logical, his preaching.
    At length, the peroration reaching,
No eye was dry: everyone sighed, lamented,
    Wept, and the tears went flowing free.
At such a sight so unexpected, he
Shed tears as well—of gladness, though!—rejoiced
    At his success; and finally, ending
His homily and, from pulpit descending,
    Said he, drying an eye still moist:
    "Brothers, for nigh an hour I've spoken,
And now methinks 'tis time for the collection.
The worker, says Saint Paul, deserves a token
Of your esteem. I pray that, on reflection,

Vous mettrez à la quête
Qui va faire le tour.
Que chacun donne ce qu'il pense...
Préparez-vous." En guise de plateau,
Il prête son chapeau,
Et la quête commence...
Elle ne rapporta rien.
On fit deux fois le tour: inutile! personne
Ne fit l'aumône.
Un homme qui prêchait si bien
Devait largement se suffire,
Sans mettre à prix le fruit des ses talents.
Le plat donc revint vide; et le prêcheur de dire:
"Je dois tous mes remerciements
A l'aimable assistance
Qui m'a rendu mon chapeau,
Avec tant d'obligeance."
Ce conte n'est pas nouveau,
Hélas! Si vous avez du talent, du génie,
Gardez-vous d'en montrer en sotte compagnie.

Each of you will recall
That for the souls of one and all
I've toiled; and will, this sacred day,
Give what, in love, he deems he may." With that,
Plateless, he chose to pass his hat,
And the collection, lo! was underway...
Empty, the hat came back. Twice more
It made the rounds; and, as before,
Nothing!... Nil!... Naught!...
Apparently the congregation thought
That one who preached so well must live
In comfort, and ought not ask one to give
A fee therefor. So it returned
Empty; whereat our theocrat
Opined: "Dear friends, at least you've earned
My thanks for giving back my hat!"
This tale is ancient, but, alas! so be it:
If you have talent, never let fools see it."

Patrie

Après huit ans écoulés dans l'absence,
Je viens revoir le ciel de mes aïeux:
Doux souvenirs de mon heureuse enfance,
Apparaissez un moment à mes yeux!

Alfred Mercier (1816–94)

Alfred Mercier numbered among the few culturally elite Creoles who, after the Civil War, devoted much of their time and talent to the preservation of the French language and literature in Louisiana. One of the most energetic of these advocates, Mercier created the literary society l'Athénée louisianais in 1876 for that purpose. *Comptes-rendus,* the organ of l'Athénée, remains one of the most important sources of francophone literature from Louisiana between 1876 and 1951. Born in 1816 to a wealthy and venerable Creole family, Mercier was sent to be educated in Paris. Although literature was his first love, he went to medical school in Paris, where he completed his degree in 1855, and then returned to New Orleans. Just before the start of the Civil War, Mercier went back to Paris, where he remained until 1865, when he returned to New Orleans and opened a medical practice. Mercier wrote all his life, and his work includes not only poetry, drama, and novels but also a variety of nonfiction, such as a treatise on yellow fever, a biography of the politician Pierre Soulé, and an essay on Creole patois. Published in 1877, his first novel, *La Fille du prêtre,* attacked the practice of celibacy in the Catholic church and provoked hostile criticism. Mercier continued to write, and in 1881 he published *L'Habitation Saint-Ybars,* an autobiographical novel about the antebellum period drawn from memories of his grandfather's plantation. Ignored for much of the past century, *L'Habitation* represents antebellum life in great detail and is particularly important for its rendering of the black Creole patois. *L'Habitation Saint-Ybars* was republished in 1982. Mercier's novel *Johnelle* (1891) treats the delicate issue of abortion in the Creole community at the turn of the century. Mercier died in New Orleans in 1894. "Fatherland" and "The Flower Moon over Louisiana" are from his first published work, *Erato,* which appeared in 1842.

Fatherland

Now, after my eight years spent countryless,
I look once more upon my fathers' skies:
Sweet memories of my childhood happiness,
I pray you loom again before my eyes!

Voici mon fleuve aux vagues solennelles:
En demi-lune il se courbe en passant,
Et la cité, comme un aiglon naissant,
A son flanc gauche étend ses jeunes ailes.

Meschacebé, tu me vis autrefois
Jouer, enfant, sur ta rive sonore;
Père des eaux, tu me revois encore
Bondir d'ivresse aux longs bruits de ta voix.

Quelle est là-bas cette maison qui tombe,
Vers le chemin qui mène à Gentilly?
Sur son front plane un silence de tombe,
Elle paraît condamnée à l'oubli.

Rien, ce n'est rien qu'un squelette sans âme
Pour l'étranger qui passe insoucieux;
Mais pour mon cœur ce toit silencieux
De jours heureux recoud toute une trame.

Sous les lambris où règne la richesse
J'ai bien souvent regretté l'air des champs;
Même à Paris jai pleuré la négresse
Qui me berçait du refrain de ses chants.

J'ai dit souvent: Oh! que ne suis-je encore
Le jeune enfant de la vieille forêt!
Oh! que ne puis-je, au réveil de l'aurore,
Voir le chasseur à partir déjà prêt!

Je me souviens de la grande harmonie
Des flots du lac qui baignaient mes pieds nus;
Là je lisais Paul et sa Virginie,
On souriait à mes pleurs ingénus.

Je hais ces murs où je suis à la gêne,
Je hais des grands le langage imposteur;
J'aime à vous voir, couché sous le vieux chêne
Cieux infinis, miroir du Créateur.

This river mine, of solemn billowings,
Flows in a half-moon curve along its bed;
The city, newborn eaglet, seems to spread,
Against the left bank, its young unfledged wings.

O Meschacebé![a] You saw me rejoice
In childish games by your resounding shore;
Father of Waters, you see me once more
Leap, drunk with joy, to hear your long-drawn voice!

What house is that, en route to Gentilly,
That crumbles and decays, now all but rotten?
The silence of the tomb hangs ponderously
About its brow, destined to stand forgotten.

What is it? Naught! A soulless skeleton
For stranger passing by without concern;
But, for my heart, that roof, now taciturn,
Knits up a skein of joyous days outspun.

In wealth's abodes, often, my thoughts turned back,
Longingly, to my fields' tranquility;
Even in Paris, I yearned for that black
Nanny, whose lullaby once cradled me.

Ofttimes I said: "Oh! Why no more am I
Child of the forest!... Oh! When wakes the day,
Why can I, once again, not saunter by
And watch the hunter, off to stalk his prey?

"I hear my echoing lake, whose waters kept
Lapping my feet: harmonies deep, immense;
There I read *Paul et Virginie,*[b] and wept
As those who watched smiled at my innocence.

"I hate these walls confining, and I hate
The speech of *grands seigneurs,* tongue counterfeit;
By old oak would I lie, and contemplate
God, mirrored in you, O heavens infinite!

Ils sont bien doux, mais qu'ils sont éphémères,
Les fruits qu'on goûte au foyer paternel!
Ravis, enfants, à l'aile de nos mères,
Sous d'autres cieux nous pleurons notre ciel.

Après huit ans écoulés dans l'absence,
Fidèle oiseau je reviens à mon nid;
Le souvenir vaut parfois l'espérance:
C'est un doux songe où l'âme rajeunit.

Douces erreurs, chimères du jeune âge,
Prismes brillants par le temps obscurcis,
Pour un moment, sur mon natal rivage,
Venez prêter un charme à mes soucis!

La Lune des Fleurs à la Louisiane

Avril

Voici l'heure paisible où l'âme se recueille:
L'oiseau silencieux repose sous la feuille,
Et des arbres divers la chevelure en fleurs
Exhale dans les airs de divines senteurs.
C'est l'heure chaste où l'âme, en ses goûts épurée,
Se berce indolemment dans un vague empyrée.
La lune, comme un phare au milieu des flots bleus,

"How sweet and short-lived are the fruits we taste
As children, by our fathers' hearth. Then, taken,
Snatched from beneath our mothers' wing, displaced,
In foreign land we mourn our land forsaken."

Now, after my eight years spent countryless,
Back to my nest, a faithful bird, I come;
Memory, at times, outweighs our hopefulness:
Sweet childhood dream, balm for soul's tedium.

Strayings of youth, illusions once sweet-seeming,
Prisms grown dull with time, that once shone fair!
Come to my native shores and, briefly gleaming,
Beguile my woe and charm my soul's despair!

a. Mercier employs here the term *Meschacebé,* the French render-
   ing of *Mississippi,* believed (as he indicates in the third stanza)
   to mean "father of waters." This popular meaning was contest-
   ed by the poet Louis Allard, who in a lengthy footnote in his
   collection *Les Epaves* argues that the correct Native American
   name for the river was *Metchasipi,* meaning the "Old Mother."
   According to *An Ojibwa Lexicon,* the word *Mississippi* is Ojib-
   wa in origin and means simply "big river." *Micca* means "be
   big" and *si:piw* means river. (In nineteenth-century texts the
   accenting of the name varied; at times it appeared with an *ac-
   cent aigue* over every *e,* and in other instances the accent ap-
   peared over the last two or simply the last.)
b. *Paul et Virginie,* a hugely popular sentimental idyll by Bernar-
   din de Saint-Pierre, was published in 1788. Saint-Pierre, a
   French naturalist and friend of Jean-Jacques Rousseau, also
   published *Etudes de la nature* in 1784. *Paul et Virginie* had an
   important influence on the romantics.

The Flower Moon over Louisiana

April

This is the peaceful time, soul's musing hour:
Silent, beneath a leaf in arbored bower,
The bird takes its repose; and flower-tressed trees
Waft their divine perfumes upon the breeze.
Now is the chaste hour when the soul, cleansed pure,
Languidly lulls itself to sleep, secure
In the empyrean's veiled domain. On high,

Brille d'un mol éclat dans l'océan des cieux;
Comme des îles d'or autour d'elle jetées,
Des étoiles sans nombre, aux flammes veloutées,
Luisent, et leur reflet semble un regard de Dieu
Qui de l'espoir éteint rallume en nous le feu.
C'est l'heure du mystère, où, par groupes unies,
Sur les ondes de l'air, dansent les Harmonies,
Où les Sylphes, amis de nos tièdes saisons,
Redescendent en chœur du sommet des maisons,
Et du vent frais, que font leurs amoureuses ailes,
Caressent les cheveux des blanches demoiselles.
Mais que vois-je glisser à l'ombre de ce mur?
Hé! Seigneur cavalier, votre pas est bien sûr!
Il arrive, il se poste, et là, sous la charmille,
Sur sa guitare il chante à quelque jeune fille.
Regardons bien.—O ciel! est-ce une vision?
Est-ce un esprit des nuits, une apparition?
Non, croyons au bonheur: Ce n'est qu'une mortelle;
Mais c'est, sur mon salut, de toutes la plus belle.
La voilà qui s'incline, et du balcon fait choir
L'échelle qui lui rend son amant chaque soir.
Heureux, cent fois heureux dans l'ombre et le mystère,
Ils vont donc oublier les soucis de la terre!
Ils vont, les yeux levés vers le pur firmament,
D'un éternel amour redire le serment,
Et, comme Juliette et celui qui l'adore,
Lorsque poindra le jour ils le diront encore!

The moon shines in the ocean of the sky,
Casting its brilliant and yet gentle light,
Like a bright beacon in the dark of night,
Over the waves; and, all about the moon,
Numberless stars of gold, like isles, lie strewn:
Their velvet glow seems like God's glance, reflected,
As hope's fire, dead in us, flares resurrected.
Now is the hour of mystery entrancing;
Time when the Harmonies go prancing, dancing
Together on air's billowing waves; time for
The summer-loving Sylphs' descent once more
From high atop our houses, to caress—
With zephyr-winged, cool, loving tenderness—
The pale-skinned damsels' tresses... Ah! But what
Is this I see, dim in the shadows, but
Gliding along the wall?... Your tread, *seigneur,*
Is sure, with neither misstep nor demur!...
Now he stops... Stands beneath the bower... And there,
Strumming on his guitar, he croons an air
To some fair maid, I know not who... But we
Need but wait, watch... Good heavens, what do I see?
A vision? Some night-fay? A sprite? A ghost?...
Happily, no! A mortal, she—the most
Beautiful, as I live and breathe, of all!...
Over the balcony she leans, lets fall
The ladder that, at every eventide,
Once again brings her lover to her side.
Happy a hundredfold are they, as thus,
Reveling in the deep, mysterious
Darkness of night, they gently put away
The cares and worldly troubles of the day.
And, with their gaze cast heavenward, they both
Plight one another their undying troth.
Like Juliet and her beau—adoring swain—
Come dawn, so shall they plight it yet again!

Le Chêne et Sa Mousse

Un enfant, au pied d'un gros chêne
Dont la barbe flottante environnait le tronc,
Dit à son père: "Pourquoi donc
Cet arbre a-t-il cette vilaine
Laine?"

Son papa répondit, pour le tirer de peine:
"C'est par un sol humide et chargé de vapeurs,
Vois-tu! mon fils, que cette mousse
Pousse.
Il n'en vient point sur les hauteurs."

Ainsi la basse Envie acharnée au Mérite,
Toujours s'y cramponnant, cherche à l'embarrasser,
Le rabaisser,
Le terrasser.
Souvent l'arbre grandit malgré son parasite.

Paul Palvadeau

Apart from publishing three poems in *Comptes-rendus de l'Athénée louisianais,* Paul Palvadeau left little trace of himself in the histories of francophone Louisiana. "The Oak and Its Moss" was first published in *Comptes-rendus* in May 1885. It was translated by Norman Shapiro for *The Fabulists French.* The moss of Palvadeau's fable is the Spanish moss characteristic of the Southeast.

The Oak and Its Moss

Beside an oak of towering size,
Whose trunk stood under billowing beards of moss,
    A child looked up with wondering eyes
        And asked, quite at a loss:
"Papa, why is this tree so full
        Of ugly wool?"
"That 'wool,'" Papa replied, to ease his mind,
    "Grows low, amid the dank morasses'
        Noxious gases.
The higher the tree, my child, the less you find."

So too does lowly Envy, clinging tight,
Beleaguer Merit, try to humble him,
        To tumble him,
        To crumble him...
The oak grows tall, and scorns his parasite.

Réponse à Mon Ami M. St. Pierre

Quand a cessé l'orage, et que le ciel plus beau
De sa robe d'azur se pare de nouveau;
Quand souriant d'espoir l'astre qui nous éclaire,
Rejette au loin son voile, et répand sa lumière;
Pour fêter le retour de ce beau jour naissant,
Le rossignol joyeux fait entendre son chant:
Ainsi puisque ta muse aujourd'hui se réveille,
Et que des sons charmants ont frappé mon oreille;
Il m'est doux de penser que du Destin jaloux,
Ton courage a vaincu le funeste courroux.
Maintenant plus d'ennuis, plus de morne silence;
Que le plaisir, ami, succède à la souffrance.
Ecarte de ton cœur ce passé ténébreux,
Que tu sus racheter par des efforts heureux;
Célèbre par tes chants cette grande victoire,
Ton retour aux vertus te couronne de gloire.

Auguste Populus

Auguste Populus, a stonemason and Creole of color, contributed three poems to *Les Cenelles*. "Reply to My Friend Monsieur St. Pierre" is a response to Michel St. Pierre's poem of gratitude, "Two Years Later"; St. Pierre's poem was dedicated to Populus, who had persuaded the suicidal St. Pierre not to take his own life (St. Pierre's poem is also included in this volume).

Auguste Populus cleverly buried a hidden meaning in "To My Friend P. Who Asked Me for My Opinion on Marriage." Read the first and third lines followed by the second and fourth lines to discover it.

Reply to My Friend Monsieur St. Pierre

When past the storm, and when, grown fair, the sky
In azure gown decks itself by and by;
When, with a smile of hope, our radiant star
Spreads everywhere its light and casts afar
Its veil; then will the nightingale at morn
Joyously sing his praise to day reborn.
Thus, since your muse wakens today anew
And charms my ear, how sweet to know that you,
Courageous, have subdued the enmity
Of a most fell and jealous Destiny.
Now no more woes, no more that silence drear;
Let pleasure thrive, let suffering disappear,
Dear friend: cast from your heart that dismal past
That, striving free, you have redeemed at last.
Celebrate now in song your triumph's story;
And may your gifts, returned, crown you with glory.

A Mon Ami P. Qui Me Demandait
Mon Opinion sur le Mariage

Dans les yeux d'une belle on peut lire aisément
La vertu, la candeur, le tendre sentiment;
L'orgueil, la vanité, l'affreuse jalousie,
Sont toujours étrangers à la femme jolie.

L'amant dans son ardeur ne sait pas deviner
Le charme par lequel il se laisse enchaîner.
Le tourment que l'amour à son âme destine
Disparaît aussitôt qu'à son tour il domine.

Ah! que l'homme a raison de s'estimer heureux
Quand il a de l'hymen serré les chastes nœuds;
Si dans le célibat il parcourt sa carrière,
La larme chaque jour vient mouiller sa paupière.

To My Friend P., Who Asked Me for My Opinion on Marriage

In a belle's eyes one can read easily
Tenderness, virtue, sweet simplicity;
Pride, vanity, and envy's bitter gall
Are, to the pretty woman, strangers all.

The lover, in his passion, cannot guess,
The charm to whose chains he must acquiesce.
The torment love reserves for him, at length,
Vanishes quickly when he shows his strength.

Ah! Man is right to think that joy is his
When, wedded by chaste bonds, the belle is his;
If evermore the bachelor's life he plies,
Each day moist tears will come and fill his eyes.

A Magda

Morte le 19 Mai 1891

I

Nous rions: tout-à-coup une aile nous effleure
Et nous fait tressaillir et nous taire. "Viens," dit
Une invisible bouche, et nous marchons. C'est l'heure
Que nulle autre ne suit sur le cadran maudit.

Léona Queyrouze (1861–1938)

Born at the beginning of the Civil War in 1861, Léona Queyrouze came of age in a New Orleans dramatically altered by the war and Reconstruction. Queyrouze was one of the most intellectually accomplished women of her generation, in large part because of her father. Léon Queyrouze, whose father had fought under Napoléon, migrated to Louisiana when he was twelve. He eventually opened a store there, importing wine and food from France. He married a Creole, Clara Tertrou, in 1857. An open-minded and intelligent man, Léon Queyrouze frequently hosted soirées with the city's intellectual elite. As a young girl Léona was permitted to attend these evening discussions, which became part of her already unorthodox education. Tutored at home, she studied, Greek, Latin, German, Spanish, mathematics, music, and even fencing. Lively, pretty, and intellectually precocious, at fifteen she befriended Lafcadio Hearn and instructed him in Creole proverbs, songs, and pronunciation during his stay in New Orleans. In 1880, at age nineteen, Léona published an essay on Racine that Hearn praised in a review. Their intellectual camaraderie led to deeper feelings that Léona expressed in a few poems published in *L'Abeille* under the pen name Constant Beauvais. Between 1884 and 1908 Léona Queyrouze published more than two dozen poems in the city's newspapers and magazines. Léona Queyrouze married Pierre-Marie-Etienne Barel in 1901. Five years before her death in 1938, she published *The Idyll: My Personal Reminiscences of Lafcadio Hearn.* "To Magda" is composed of three sonnets that begin by expressing the personal grief over the death of a child and move to the more public mourning over the massacre of eleven prison inmates by a mob of the city's outraged citizens.

For Magda

Died May 19, 1891

I

We laugh... and suddenly a wing flits past,
Grazes us, and we shudder silently.
"Come," says an unseen mouth, as tolls the last
Hour in time's cursèd clockwise round; and we

Et tandis que ta lèvre, à ta mère qui pleure,
Encore souriait, peut-être en cette nuit
Où l'œil de l'esprit voit, cherchais-tu la demeure
Des absents bien-aimés. Ton âme qui nous fuit

A doucement roulé du sein chaud de ta mère
Aux bras tendus là-bas. Tu t'en vas la première
De celles que j'aimais, fille de mon ami.

Espoir, déception, réalité, chimère,
Ne se repaîtront plus de ton cœur endormi.
Tu ne tremperas plus, à notre coupe amère,

II

Ta lèvre ardente et pure. Avant moi tu verras
Ces fils d'un autre temps qui furent nos ancêtres,
Ils étaient fiers et grands; tu les reconnaîtras.
Alors, dans ce séjour où, sans crainte des traîtres,

On peut enfin dormir, enfant, tu leur diras:
"C'est l'instant du réveil. On a besoin, ô maîtres!
"De vos âmes sans peur et de vos puissants bras.
"Levez-vous: l'heure presse."—Et tu verras ces êtres

De granit et d'airain, à ta voix tressaillir,
Et de leurs yeux taris des pleurs de feu jaillir,
Lorsqu'ils écouteront le récit de carnage,

D'infamie et d'horreur.[a] Tous, ils se lèveront!
Mais quand tu leur diras que le sombre engrenage
Pour ressorts eut leurs fils, tous ils retomberont!

III

O pardon, si les cris de mon cœur révolté
Vont troubler ton repos! A toi le calme immense
Et radieux. A moi le rêve et sa démence,
Les sommeils douloureux et la terne clarté

Du doute. Je voulais dire à tous ta beauté,
Ton charme et ton parfum, douce fleur de clémence
Et d'amour. Mais hélas! dès que mon chant commence,
Il hésite et s'égare, et, bientôt arrêté,

Move on... Your mother, weeping, watched you cast
A lingering smile upon her: can it be
That, with the spirit's eye, through the dark, vast,
You sought lost loves, flown to eternity?

Your soul rolled gently from her warming breast
Into their arms... Of all whom I loved best,
You, dear friend's daughter, are the first to part!

Dashed hopes, reality, phantasmal quest—
No more shall these feed on your sleeping heart;
Nor will you sip life's goblet, woe-possessed,

II

With lips pure, passionate. Before me, you
Will see our forebears, sons of times gone by—
Ancestors proud—in death's domain, and who
Fear now no traitors' villainy, but lie

At last in peaceful sleep; and, child, thereto
Will you declare: "Masters! The hour draws nigh
To hie yourselves awake! We need, anew,
Your dauntless souls and doughty arms! Come, fly!"

Then will you see those bronze and granite shades
Quake at your words, and tears, in flame cascades,
Flow from their eyes. When you tell them the fell,

Foul carnage wrought, up will rise one and all!
But when you say it was their sons, pell-mell,
Who twisted taut the springs, down will they fall!

III

Pardon me, pray, if my heart's anguished shout
Troubles your rest. Yours is the calm, immense
And radiant; mine, dream's bedlam, consequence
Of pain-wracked slumber and of faint-lit doubt.

It was to sing your charms that I set out
To write my verse, that all might quaff the scents
Of your love's tender bloom; but, starting thence,
Soon I would stray, and stop, and turn about.

Change ses doux accents en un sombre délire:
Car un souffle fatal a passé sur ma lyre.
En place du sanglot vient le rugissement.

Non, je ne puis pleurer et ne sais plus sourire.
Toi qui dors dans l'extase et l'éblouissement,
Pardonne, je t'aimais, et ne puis que le dire.

Nouvelle Orléans, le 20 mai 1891

In somber wise my sighs and sobs gave way
To roar and bellowing. My lyre would play
One note alone: one breath filled death's abyss—

No smile, no tear. And so, sadly, I pray
You pardon me, in your resplendent bliss...
I loved you. Now, no more is there to say.

New Orleans, May 20, 1891

---

a. Queyrouze alludes to the prison massacre of March 14, 1891, when a mob of outraged citizens broke into the Old Parish Prison and murdered eleven of the nineteen Italians being held in connection with the assassination of Police Chief David Hennessey in October 1890. The accused had been aquitted, but it was widely known that Mafia money had "bought" the jury. Hennessey had been investigating Mafia activities in New Orleans when he was murdered. The incident provoked strong protests from the Italian government, and in December 1891 President Benjamin Harrison went before the Congress to denounce the mob action and authorized monetary compensation for the victims' families. None of the vigilantes was ever arrested or charged.

Amour et Dévouement

A Miss Ida B. Wells

Tout pour l'humanité! tout pour Dieu! rien pour soi!
Telle est, du dévouement, l'inextinguible foi!
      Pour calmer la blessure,
Pour essuyer des pleurs, protéger l'orphelin,
Etouffer l'injustice et braver l'assassin,
      Il faut une âme sûre!

Pour quelle noble cause, ô divine harmonie,
A tes feux je viens retremper mon génie!
      Un [bel] ange des Cieux
Parut à l'horizon! Et sa race flétrie,
Veut que ma faible plume en ce jour lui dédie
      Ce chant élogieux.

Jadis, en Béthulie, une vierge candide
Comme toi, pour les siens devint fière, intrépide;
      Et le nom de Judith

Victor-Ernest Rillieux (1842–98)

Born in New Orleans in 1842, Victor Rillieux was a Creole of color and the younger brother of the illustrious inventor Norbert Rillieux. Although Victor was a prolific writer of poetry, satirical songs, and odes, much of his work has been lost. Rillieux, who was blind, died in 1898. Rodolphe Desdunes included "The Coward" in his history of the Creoles of color, *Nos hommes et notre histoire.* Rillieux's ode to Ida B. Wells, "Love and Devotion," apparently first appeared in print in Maceo Coleman's *Creole Voices* (1945). Ida B. Wells was a courageous black woman who devoted her career as a journalist to exposing lynching in the South. Rillieux's poem speaks to the sense that Creoles of color shared a plight with the newly freed bondsmen and -women.

Love and Devotion

For Miss Ida B. Wells

Selfless to serve God and the human race:
Such, faith's devotion that naught can efface!
    To calm wounds' agony,
Dry tears, suppress injustices, protect
The orphan, hold the vile assassin checked,
    The soul must stalwart be!

For what fine cause, O harmony divine,
I temper in your fires this talent mine!
    A heavenly angel fair
Stood tall against the sky; and her reviled
Race asks that my poor pen, for this pure child,
    Compose a paean's air.

In days of old, a maid—guileless, like you—
To save her people in Bethulia, grew
    Dauntless and bold. Her name?

Terrassant Holopherne, aux murs de la patrie,
Arriva jusqu'à nous! Et sa gloire infinie
  Brille encore au Zénith.

Quelques siècles plus tard, au beau pays de France,
Le peuple, en deuil, demande à Dieu sa délivrance:
  Jeanne d'Arc apparaît!
Vierge, elle est invincible, aux combats elle vole!
Du haut de son bûcher l'éternelle auréole
  Lance un brillant attrait!

Mais toi, vierge au teint brun, au pays du Sauvage,
Par la voix, tu combats! Puis, comme en un mirage,
  Ton cœur, au premier rang
Fait briller le flambeau de la noble phalange
Sans laisser sur les sols qu'effleurent tes pas d'ange:
  Un long sillon de sang.

Oh! jamais! car ta race, abhorrant tous les crimes,
Des deux rôles, choisit le rôle des victimes
  A celui des bandits
Dont les rifles, le lynch, le bûcher, la potence
Et les sombres forfaits sont par l'intolérance,
  Dans tout le Sud bénits.

Parle donc! Que l'élan de ton âme oppressée
Redise, sans détours, à l'Europe froissée,
  L'horrible sort des tiens
Que la jeune Amérique, adepte du supplice,
Immole, chaque jour, au dieu de l'injustice!
  Idole des païens!

Judith et Jeanne d'Arc illuminent ta route!
Déjà le White Cap s'émeut et [te] redoute;
  Mais pour son Ida Wells,
Un peuple valeureux, courbé par la souffrance,
Implore avec amour de la Toute-puissance
  Les bienfaits éternels.

Judith, who Holofernes slew, beside
The city wall: forever glorified.
      Writ in the stars, her fame!

Centuries pass, and in France—beauteous nation—
Bereaved, the people seek God's liberation.
      Lo! Joan of Arc appears!
Virgin invincible, she routs the foe,
And, from the stake, her halo's flame, aglow,
      Eternal, lights the years!

But you, O virgin brown of skin, and who
Dwell in the Brute's wild land, with words you do
      Your deeds, for freedom's sake.
Your vanguard heart holds high the burning brand,
And your soft angel tread, over the land,
      Leaves no blood in its wake.

No! Never! For your race all crime abhors,
And would elect the victim's role as yours,
      And not the villain's, whose
Lynchings, guns, gallows, stakes make manifest
That arrogance throughout the Southland blessed,
      And sins of gloomiest hue!

Speak then! Let your oppressed soul shriek, cry out,
And let Europe, distressed, have little doubt
      About the fate abject
Of those a young America, each day—
Expert at torture!—immolates to pay
      A heathen god respect!

May Joan of Arc and Judith light your path!
The White Hoods cower, fearing that your wrath
      Your victory foretells;
And folk courageous, loving, bowed in woe,
Entreat eternal God, that He bestow
      His gifts on Ida Wells!

Le Timide

Chaque jour, je la vois, charmante, gracieuse,
Au milieu de ses fleurs, sous l'oranger fleuri;
Mais quand de son doux chant la note harmonieuse
Vient raviver les feux de mon cœur attendri,
Pourquoi, timide, il faut qu'en mon ivresse extrême
Je ne puisse jamais dire à celle que j'aime:
             Chante toujours,
             O mes amours!
          Chante, chante toujours?

Ravi, brûlant d'amour à ses côtés, j'admire
Ses grâces, sa beauté, son regard enchanteur;
Pourtant, quand de sa lèvre un suave sourire,
Comme un reflet du Ciel vient embraser mon cœur,
Pourquoi, timide et faible, en mon extase même
Je n'ose dire, hélas! à la dive que j'aime:
             Souris toujours
             O mes amours!
          Souris, souris toujours?

Le soir dans son hamac, j'aime à la voir rêveuse.
Oh! quand elle murmure, en un souffle amoureux
Un nom, un tendre aveu qu'en mon âme joyeuse
J'écoute, avec amour, comme un chant des Cieux;
Pourquoi, croyant, doutant, à ce moment suprême,
Je ne puisse, oh! mon Dieu, dire à l'ange que j'aime:
             Rêve toujours,
             O mes amours!
          Rêve, rêve toujours?

The Coward

Each day I see her—charming, graceful child—
Beneath the orange tree, by flowers surrounded;
But when her voice sings to my heart, beguiled,
Breathing to life its passion-flames, confounded,
Why must I—cowardly—but yearn the more,
Nor ever tell this one that I adore:
>"Sing, sing to me
>Eternally!
>Sing, O my love, to me!"

Burning with love beside her, I admire
Her beauty, grace, enchanting glance, her smile;
But as upon her velvet lips the fire
Of Heaven, reflected, sears my heart the while,
Why, weak and timid, dare I not implore
This goddess whom, ecstatic, I adore:
>"Smile, smile on me
>Eternally!
>Smile, O my love, on me!"

At dusk I love to watch as, swaying, she
Dreams in her hammock, sighing, murmuring
A name... A sweet confession that, for me,
Is like a song I hear God's Heavens sing:
Why can I not—moment supreme!—restore
My faith, and tell this angel I adore:
>"Dream, dream of me
>Eternally!
>Dream, O my love, of me!"

Rondeau redoublé

Aux Francs Amis

De francs amis demandent un rondeau.
Allons, ma muse, il faut faire merveille!
N'écrivons plus désormais pour de l'eau,
De bon vin vieux on nous paiera bouteille.

Pour t'obtenir, ô doux jus de la treille!—
Il faut rimer dans un genre nouveau,
Il ne faut pas ici que je sommeille,
De francs amis demandent un rondeau.

De vin Bacchus nous promet un tonneau,
De fleurs l'Amour nous offre une corbeille;
Du dieu du vin j'aime mieux le cadeau,
Allons, ma muse, il faut faire merveille!

La nuit souvent pour écrire je veille,
Au jour, mes vers tombent dans l'eau; c'est beau!
Dès à présent, muse, je te conseille,
N'écrivons plus désormais pour de l'eau.

Nicol Riquet

Only a few facts are known about the life and death of Nicol Riquet—among them that he was a Creole of color and cigar maker in New Orleans. (The unusual spelling of his first name appears consistently in all references.) Riquet was well known for songs such as the "Double Rondeau," which was published in *Les Cenelles*. The Francs Amis, translated here as the "Loyal Band," was a society of Creoles of color.

Double Rondeau

For the Loyal Band

My loyal band wants a rondeau from me.
So come, let us work wonders, muse of mine!
No more shall water be my destiny:
They vow to treat me to a fine old wine.

To earn you, though—O sweet juice of the vine!—
In new form must I rhyme my minstrelsy.
No time to rest, all sleep must I decline:
My loyal band wants a rondeau from me.

Bacchus has sworn to let the wine flow free;
Cupid has promised fair bouquets and fine—
The former gift will the more welcome be!—
So come, let us work wonders, muse of mine!

Often, at night, line upon sleepless line
I write; come morn, I fling them in the sea!
Henceforth, O muse, I pray you change design:
No more shall water be my destiny.

Je sens sortir du fond de mon cerveau
Un nouveau vers à rime sans pareille;
Allons toujours, nous ferons un tableau:
De bon vin vieux on nous paiera bouteille.

A la censure, hélas! qui nous surveille,
Vite en passant ôtons notre chapeau,
A ses discours ouvrons bien notre oreille
Pour n'être pas nommé poètereau—
        De francs amis.

Deep in my brain I feel new poesy
Spring forth, new rhyme that will all else outshine;
The very picture, we, of jollity:
They vow to treat me to a fine old wine.

As for the censors—dour and unbenign,
Alas!—let's tip our cap at them as we
Pass by, and lend an ear, lest they opine
A wretched rhymester shares your company,
      My loyal band.

Adrien Rouquette (1813–87)

Among the most remarkable of Louisiana's Creoles was Adrien
Rouquette. One of five children, Adrien was the second son of Do-
minique, a Frenchman from Bordeaux, and Louise Cousin, a Creole. Although
Dominique Rouquette père operated a wine business in New Orleans, he set-
tled his family in Bayou Saint-James. Adrien grew up near a settlement of
Choctaws and spent much of his childhood in their company. Fearing that her
son's affection for the Choctaw might be harmful (he became fluent in the lan-
guage), Madame Rouquette sent Adrien to a school in Kentucky where he
studied English. By the time he reached sixteen, both his parents had died,
and Adrien decided to follow his older brother, also named Dominique, to
Paris, where he continued his education. In 1833, after four years in France,
Adrien returned to New Orleans. He was never at ease in the city, however,
and soon returned to the bayou and the Choctaws. Adrien's affection for the
Choctaw determined his extraordinary career. He returned to New Orleans
to study for the priesthood. In 1844 he was ordained a Catholic priest and
became the first Creole to take holy orders after the Louisiana Purchase in 1803.
Well known to be an eloquent speaker, Father Rouquette's sermons took on
an abolitionist tone by 1850. In fact, he longed to have a ministry among the

Promenade du Soir sur la Levée

Oh! respectez mes jeux et ma faiblesse,
Vous qui savez le secret de mon cœur
Oh! laissez-moi, pour unique richesse,
De l'eau dans une fleur,
L'air frais du soir...

—Dovalle

Me voilà cheminant, le soir sur la *Levée*,
L'œil à terre baissé, l'âme au ciel élevée!
Plus de hâve irlandais, de rouge matelot,
Qui roule le baril, ou pousse le ballot;,
Plus de ces *drays* pesants, à la chaîne bruyante,
Qui voilent le soleil de poussière étouffante;

158

Choctaw, and after fourteen years of service in New Orleans, he had his request granted. A malaria epidemic swept through the region during the Civil War, and access to quinine was limited. Knowing the possible impact on the Choctaw, Adrien Rouquette did what should have been impossible. He persuaded Admiral Farragut to give him the quinine necessary for the Choctaws and prevented the decimation of their community. The Choctaw called him "Chahta-Ima," meaning "One of us."

Adrien Rouquette may have been the most self-consciously Louisianian of the early Creole poets. He was a prolific writer, and unlike many of his fellow Louisianians, he wrote in both French and English. His volumes of poetry include *Les Savanes: poésies américaines* (1844) and *Wild Flowers* (1848), and several uncollected poems appeared in *Renaissance louisianaise, Comptes-rendus,* and *Le Meschacébé.* In 1879 he published *La Nouvelle Atala,* a Native American legend, in part as a response to Chateaubriand's *Atala.* Adrien Rouquette died in New Orleans in 1887. Of the poems included here, "An Evening Stroll on the Levee," and "Recollection of Kentucky" are especially evocative of the "new" world. All four poems are from *Les Savanes.*

Evening Stroll on the Levee

> Honor my weakness and my pastime's pleasure,
> O you who know my heart's most secret thought!
> Grant me the flower's dew; no other treasure
>   Have I desired or sought,
> Save dusk's cool air...
>
>   —Dovalle[a]

This evening, on the levee, here I stroll,
Eye turned toward earth, and heavenward my soul;
No pale-skinned Irish lads, no sailors red
Of countenance, hauling the bales outspread,
Rolling huge kegs; none of those heavy drays,
Clanging with chains and veiling, in a haze

Mais la foule, au bruit sourd, ce flot calme et mouvant,
Qui cause et qui regarde un navire arrivant;
Le gros négociant, l'âme tout inquiète,
Qui cherche à lire au loin: *Salem,* ou *Lafayette;*
La mère, qui vient voir s'il arrive un enfant;
L'ami, s'il vient à bord un ami qu'il pressent;
Le marchand qui, cupide, attend ses modes neuves,
Modes de jeune fille et d'oublieuses veuves;
Et tandis que groupés, et dans l'anxiété,
Ceux-ci pleins de tristesse, et ceux-là de gaîté,
Ils causent, moi, je passe; et, poursuivant mon rêve,
Je m'en vais, parcourant la longue et blanche grève;
Contemplant, tour à tour, les bois et le ciel bleu;
Jetant mes vers au fleuve, et ma prière à Dieu!

1837

L'Homme, Oiseau de Passage sur la Terre

Such is the glorious independence of man in a savage state!

—W. Irving

Non, les plus opulentes villes ne pourraient procurer à mon
cœur autant de plaisirs que les simples beautés de la nature,
dont je jouissais librement dans ce sauvage lieu.

—Daniel Boone

A M. D——— R———

Frère, j'ai lu tes vers: douce et fraîche rosée,
Ils ont rendu la sève à mon âme épuisée:
Et, pourtant, je suis triste! en ces jours si mauvais
Je ne sais où je suis, je ne sais où je vais:
Coquille, que la vague a jetée au rivage,
J'entends gronder le bruit de l'Océan sauvage:

Of stifling dust, the sun; only the low
Murmuring throng, a gently moving flow
Of folk come here to watch a boat about
To moor... Anxious, the trader—stolid, stout—
Peering up river at its silhouette
("Is it *The Salem?* or *The Lafayette?*"...);
The mother, come, hoping to greet her son;
The friend, meeting a long-expected one;
The money-hungry merchant waiting there
For the new styles the stylish belles will wear,
And widows who their mourning have put by...
And, while all wait and cast an anxious eye,
Chatting and chattering—some sad, some gay—
Over the long white strand I wend my way,
Skirting the river, drawn on by the dream
That haunts me, as I toss into the stream—
Gazing upon the woods, the azure air—
These verses mine, and unto God, my prayer.

1837

---

a. The epigraph is from a poem entitled "Le Sylphe," by
   Charles Dovalle (1807–29), a French romantic poet.

Man, Bird of Passage on This Earth

Such is the glorious independence of man in a
savage state!

—Washington Irving[a]

No populous city, with all the varieties of
commerce and stately structures, could afford
so much pleasure to my mind, as the beauties of
nature I found here.

—Daniel Boone[b]

For Monsieur D—— R——

Brother, I read your poem: like soft dew
It made the sap rise in my soul anew—
My oh so withered soul! Yet sad am I,
These days; for me, alas, all turns awry:

Météore, égaré de sa route d'azur,
Je tourne, en chancelant, sur un axe moins sûr...
    Oh! que je voudrais donc me créer une vie
Dans quelque coin de terre ignoré de l'Envie:
Loin du bruit qui nous trouble au sein de la cité,
Comme Daniel Boon, dans un désert jeté:
Et, comme lui, courant, libre dans mon domaine!
    O Boon! ô vieux chasseur! que de fois m'ont souri
Ton chien et ta cabane, au bord du Missouri;
Que de fois m'ont souri, dans ma tristesse amère,
Ta Bible et ton fusil, ton calme et ta prière;
Tes haltes sous tout arbre, et ta course en tout lieu;
Ton mépris de nos biens, et ton amour pour Dieu!
    Oui; mais, jeune alcyon, sous la natale zone,
A tout souffle orageux je tends mon aile jaune;
Et, traînant mon nid d'algue au bord de l'Océan,
Je crie; impatient, j'appelle l'ouragan!...
    C'est que je ne suis pas un oiseau de la grève:
Tout flot qui nous emporte, est le flot que je rêve!
Oui, brille à l'horizon la voile d'un vaisseau;
Vibre en l'air quelque chant de voyageur oiseau;
Vienne, vienne le vent, la tempête sublime:
Et l'on verra flotter l'alcyon sur l'abîme!
    Ah! luise au loin surtout le phare de Sion,
L'étoile de la croix; et, joyeux alcyon,
On verra le chrétien, ouvrant enfin son aile,
Voler de cette vie à la vie éternelle;
Abandonner ce globe, avec calme et dédain;
Et, planant au-dessus du céleste jardin,
Saluer de sa voix la mystique patrie,
Dieu, les anges, les saints, les élus et Marie!

    Nouvelle-Orléans, 1837

I know not where I am, whither I go,
Nor why... A shell the ocean's ebb and flow
Has tossed ashore, I hear its savage howl;
Lost in the blue, a meteor run afoul,
I twist and turn with no fixed center sure...

Oh, that I might go live in some fair, pure
Corner of earth that Envy cannot spoil:
Far from the city's bosom, with its broil
And bustle, wandering free, like Daniel Boone!
Off in the wilds, with none to importune,
Oppress me, in my own demesne, I could,
Exiled from Mankind, do as do I would.

O Boone, old hunter! Ah! How often your
Dog and your cabin, by Missouri's shore,
Have smiled upon me; and how often, too,
In my bitter despondency, have you
Smiled on me, rifle and your Bible in hand,
In prayerful calm, by any tree whatever;
You and your endless quest, forsaking never,
Scorning man's wealth, by love of God pressed on!...

Yes... But here, in my land, young halcyon,
I reach my yellow wings to east, to west,
With each storm's gust... Dragging my seaweed nest
Unto the Ocean's shore, impatiently,
I beg for the hurricane to succor me!

For no land bird am I, well satisfied
To haunt the strand: whatever flowing tide
Will bear me off, to any land... Ah yes,
That is the tide I dream of, limitless!
Let the horizon shine with distant sail;
Let the bird-traveler's song trill on the gale;
Let but the tempest roar, sublime, and this
Halcyon will soar above the vast abyss!

But, more than that, let Zion's beacon glow—
The cross's shining star—and, at last, lo!
There will you see this Christian soul prepare—
This halcyon, joyous—to take to the air;
And, wings outspread, and with a calm disdain,
Leaving this sphere behind, this drear domain,
Fly off to life eternal, high above

Souvenir du Kentucky

Kentucky, the bloody land!

Le Seigneur dit à Osée: "Après cela, néanmoins,
Je l'attirerai doucement à moi, je l'amènerai dans
la solitude, et je lui parlerai au cœur."

—Osée

Enfant, je dis un soir: Adieu, ma bonne mère!
Et je quittai gaîment sa maison et sa terre.
Enfant, dans mon exil, une lettre, un matin,
(O Louise!) m'apprit que j'étais orphelin!
Enfant, je vis les bois du Kentucky sauvage,
Et l'homme se souvient des bois de son jeune âge!
Ah! dans le Kentucky les arbres sont bien beaux:
C'est la *terre de sang,* aux indiens tombeaux,
Terre aux belles forêts, aux séculaires chênes,
Aux bois suivis de bois, aux magnifiques scènes;
Imposant cimetière, où dorment en repos
Tant de *rouges-tribus* et tant de *blanches-peaux;*
Où l'ombre du vieux Boon, immobile génie,
Semble écouter, la nuit, l'éternelle harmonie,
Le murmure éternel des immenses déserts,
Ces mille bruits confus, ces mille bruits divers,
Cet orgue des forêts, cet orchestre sublime,
O Dieu! que seul tu fis, que seul ton souffle anime!
Quand au vaste clavier pèse un seul de tes doigts,
Soudain, roulent dans l'air mille flots à la fois;
Soudain, au fond des bois, sonores basiliques,

The heavenly garden; and, with song of love,
Bow to his soul's true land, made manifest:
God, angels, saints, and Mary's chosen blest!

New Orleans, 1837

---

a. From Washington Irving's book *A Tour on the
   Prairies* (1835). The poem is dedicated to A. Rouquette's
   brother Dominique.
b. The remark is from *The Adventures of Colonel Daniel
   Boone* (1793). Adrien Rouquette greatly admired the
   frontiersman Daniel Boone (1734–1820).

Recollection of Kentucky

Kentucky, the bloody land![a]

"Therefore, behold, I will allure her, and
bring her into the wilderness,and speak
comfortably unto her."

—Hosea 2:14

Mere child, one night I said a last farewell
And gaily left my mother's side, to dwell
No more within her house, her native land.
Mere child, one morning, writ in sorrow's hand
I read a letter (O Louise!), and knew
That, exiled, now was I an orphan too…
Mere child, I wandered through Kentucky's wild,
Unconquered nature… Ah! When, but a child,
One sees the forest's beauty, never can
The memory fade when he grows to a man!…
Kentucky!… Oh, what sylvan wonders these!
The Indian tombs, *the bloody land,* the trees—
Those venerable oaks, wood after wood
That, there, for countless centuries have stood
In grandeur! Graveyard, vast expanse, where those
Redskins and those *Pale Faces,* too, repose
In peace; where old Boone's spirit—motionless
Shade—seems, in night's great wasteland emptiness,
To listen to the harmonies, dark sounds'
Eternal murmurings, as there resounds,
In myriad tones, that sublime symphony,

Bourdonne un océan de sauvages musiques;
Et l'homme, à tous ces sons de l'orgue universel,
L'homme tombe à genoux, en regardant le ciel!
Il tombe, il croit, il prie; et, chrétien sans étude,
Il retrouve, étonné, Dieu dans la solitude!

1838

Aux Dames de la Nouvelles-Orléans[a]

C'est un malheur d'être pauvre mais c'est un malheur
plus grand encore d'être un mauvais riche.

—Saint Grégoire de Nazianze

Le plaisir de donner est incomparable et infini,
puisqu'il est divin.

—Champion de Pontalier

Dans la salle de bal, dans la salle splendide
Où tant de fois a lui votre regard limpide,
Où le front ruisselant de reflets lumineux
Vous avez tant de fois promené vos grands yeux;
Dans la splendide salle, oh! vous accourrez toutes
Par des motifs divers et par diverses routes;
Oh! oui, vous y viendrez, que ce soit par orgueil,
Folie ou vanité, triple et funeste écueil!
Ou que ce soit plutôt par l'amour seul poussées,
Vous viendrez consoler ces filles délaissées!
Vous viendrez secourir celles qu'en leur bonté
Adoptèrent pour Dieu les Sœurs de Charité,
Ces enfants que l'Eglise abrite sous son aile,
L'Eglise, cette mère adorable, immortelle!
Oh! oui, vous qui croyez au céleste trésor,
Chrétiennes accourez et prodiguez votre or;

That forest organ that, O God! can be
No other's work but yours alone, you who
Alone can breathe its pipes to life!... When you
Press but one key, in sudden gush the air
Floods in a mighty rushing sea; and there
Tree-temples echo with the pulse and pound
Of nature's music, all the woods around.
Man hears the organ's heavenly melodies,
Gazes above, believes, falls to his knees—
Christian uncomplicated—prays... And, awed,
In solitude once more he finds his God!

1838

---

a. Rouquette attributes this remark to Boone and included a
   lengthy footnote on him in *Les Savanes.*

To the Ladies of New Orleans[a]

It is woeful to be a poor man; but to be an evil
rich man is more woeful still.

—Saint Gregory Nazianzen[b]

The pleasure in giving is incomparable and
infinite, *since it is divine.*

—Champion de Pontalier[c]

In this resplendent hall, this great hall, where
Your limpid glance so often sparkled fair;
Where, brows a-glisten with light's mirrored rays,
Your large eyes have so often cast their gaze;
In this resplendent hall, ah! you will come
By different routes, for different reasons. Some,
Will come through folly, vanity, or pride—
Each one a deadly reef beneath the tide!
Rather, be drawn by love: love for those left
Behind by life, orphans, of love bereft!
Rather, be drawn to help these poor souls whom
The blessèd nuns bear from the Church's womb
And give to God: Sisters of Charity,
Who place these young girls, from their misery,
Safe in the refuge of their Mother's wing—
The Church eternal! Ah, yes! Come! Come bring

Ouvrez, ouvrez vos mains, pieuses Desdémones;
Versez sans regarder d'abondantes aumônes;
Versez, versez, ô vous dont le cœur maternel
Sème ici-bas le bien pour recueillir au ciel!
Et vous, brunes beautés, vous, rêveuses créoles,
Vous qui lisez aussi les saintes paraboles:
Oh! venez et donnez; donnez beaucoup ou peu;
Car donner, voyez-vous, c'est ressembler à Dieu!
Donnez, car en donnant toute femme est bien belle!
Toute femme en donnant a quelque ange près d'elle!
Donnez, car en donnant au pauvre on s'enrichit;
En donnant à Lazare on donne à Jésus-Christ!

1840

---

a. Ces vers ont été composés à l'occasion d'une foire en
   faveur des orphelines, qui a eu lieu dans la grande salle de bal
   de la Bourse nouvelle.

Your gold, you, Christian ladies, who believe
In wealth celestial! Let these waifs receive
Abundant alms at your unstinting hand.
Bestow like pious Desdemonas, and
Give! Give! Count not how much, O you whose heart
Maternal sows the seed to reap your part
Of heaven's harvest! And you, Creole belles,
Dark-skinned, who, dreaming, read what Scripture tells
In sacred parable: give! Your reward
Will be your living likeness to Our Lord!
For, giving, woman grows in beauty! Give,
That by your side an angel pure may live!
Yes, more you give the poor, more you possess:
Give Lazarus, and you give Christ no less!

1840

---

a. These verses were composed on the occasion of a benefit for young
orphan girls that took place in the grand ballroom of the new Stock
Exchange.
b. Gregory Nazianzen (330–ca. 390) was a theologian and eloquent
speaker whose legacy includes forty-five sermons, letters, and poetry.
c. The remark is from François Champion de Pontalier (1731–1812), in
Variétés d'un philosophe provincial (1767).

[François-] Dominique Rouquette

(1810–90)

The elder brother of Father Adrien Rouquette, François-Dominique Rouquette was born in Bayou Lacombe, Louisiana, to a French father and a Creole mother in 1810. Bayou Lacombe was remote, peopled primarily by the indigenous Choctaw. The Rouquette brothers learned the Choctaw's language early on and preferred their company over that of other Creole children. At age twelve Dominique was sent to school in Nantes, France. By the time he returned to New Orleans in 1828, his mother had passed away. Refusing to study law in Philadelphia, Dominique returned to Bayou Lacombe. Between 1836 and 1838 Dominique Rouquette made two separate trips to Paris, and his first collection of poetry, *Meschacébéennes,* was published there in 1839. Another collection of poetry, *Fleurs d'Amérique,* was published in New Orleans in 1857. Rouquette's many poems also appeared in *Comptes-rendus* and in several of the city's newspapers, including *La Chronique* and *La Revue.*

Unlike Adrien, Dominique Rouquette led a chaotic and unlucky life. In 1848 he opened a school in New Orleans, and when this failed, he took his young family to Arkansas in an attempt to make his fortune. Every practical venture

Imitation de l'Allemand.

Je rêvais, ô blonde vermeille,
Que tu sommeillais au tombeau;
Je pleurais... soudain je m'éveille,
Et mes pleurs coulaient de nouveau.

Je rêvais, ô blonde vermeille,
Que ton cœur m'avait oublié;
Je pleurais... soudain je m'éveille;
Et mes pleurs long-temps ont coulé.

Dominique Rouquette undertook failed, however; when he became unable to support them, his wife took their children and returned to her own family. After her death Rouquette sent his children to live with his nephew Cyprien Dufour, who then raised them. A pathetic figure in his later years and virtually homeless, Dominique Rouquette became a sort of wandering minstrel even though his peregrinations never took him beyond the parishes around New Orleans. Toward the end of his life, Natalie, a well-educated woman of color, made a place for him in her home. (Natalie may have been Natalie Populus Mello, a Creole of color, an educator, and a journalist. Educated at Sainte-Barbe Academy, she later became principal of the Couvent School.) Rouquette died in 1890; he was eighty years old. The poems included here are from his *Fleurs d'Amérique*. Ranging thematically from the natural charm of the bayou in "The Whipoorwill," to the triumphant boast of "For Monsieur Hilarion Huc," to the comic jibes of "The Bachelor," Rouquette's verses, in content and form, are wonderfully evocative of mid-nineteenth-century Louisiana.

Imitation from the German[a]

I dreamt, O blonde of reddish hue,
That in the grave entombed you slept;
I cried... Then, waking, I came to,
And my tears once again I wept.

I dreamt, O blonde of reddish hue,
That your heart had forgotten me;
I cried... Then, waking, I came to,
And my tears flowed unceasingly.

Je rêvais, ô blonde vermeille,
Que tu me gardais tes amours:
Songe heureux! soudain je m'éveille:
Et mes larmes coulaient toujours.

Nouvelle-Orléans, 1839

Le Whip-Poor-Will

Des bois américains plaintive philomèle,
Dont le chant aux soupirs de la brise se mêle,
Dont les accords touchants assoupissent le cœur;
De nos nuits sans sommeil tendre consolateur,
Oh! viens, lorsque tout dort en cette solitude,
Viens, *poor-will,* te poser sur ma hutte d'étude;
Viens: après les ardeurs et tous les bruits du jour,
Après toutes ces voix qui conseillent l'amour,
Toutes ces voix d'oiseaux qui m'amollissent l'âme,
Après ces bruits, ces voix, ces chants d'épithalame,
Il me faut, pour calmer la fièvre de mes sens,
Tes plaintes; tes soupirs, baume des cœurs souffrans.

avril 1840

A un Enfant

> Ne faites pas de bruit autour de cette tombe;
> Laissez l'enfant dormir et la mère pleurer!
>
> —Victor Hugo

Enfant! je t'enviais, lorsque mon œil morose,
De tristesse glacé, te contemplait, un jour,

I dreamt, O blonde of reddish hue,
That mine was all the love you bore:
Sweet dream!... Then, waking, I came to,
And my tears flowed forevermore.

New Orleans, 1839

---

a. The "imitation" is of a Heinrich Heine poem from
   the *Lyrisches Intermezzo* (1827): "Ich hab im Traum
   geweinet, / Mir träumte, du lägest im Grab . . ."
   The original was set to music by several composers,
   most notably Franz Schubert in his *Dichterliebe*.

The Whippoorwill

You, like the nightingale,[a] O denizen
Of forest deeps, woodlands American,
Whose song blends with the sighing of the breeze,
Who soothe the heart with plaintive harmonies;
You, who console our sleepless nights, I pray
You come and sing my solitude away,
Perched by my cabin-study; come, "Poor Will,"
While everything about lies sleeping, still.
After the heat of day, the noise, all those
Who, urging me to love, give no repose;
Birds that beset my soul with earnest prayers!
After those voices, noises, wedding-airs,
My fevered senses need the gentling calm
Of your laments: the suffering heart's sweet balm.

April 1840

---

a. The author seems, curiously, to be equating the North
   American whippoorwill with the nightingale, known in
   classical mythology as Philomela.

For a Child

I pray you make no noise about this grave;
Let sleep the child, and let the mother weep.

—Victor Hugo[a]

Dear child! Oh, how I envied you one day,
When my woe-frozen glance gazed on you there,

Comme un frêle bouton qui s'attache à la rose,
Endormi sur un sein chaste et vierge d'amour.

Maintenant, maintenant encore je t'envie!
Car Dieu, dans sa bonté, trésor mystérieux,
Ange, t'amnistia de l'exil de la vie:
Je t'enviais sur terre et je t'envie aux cieux!

Ah! ne sois point ingrat! souviens-toi de ta mère,
De ta famille en pleurs t'invoquant à genoux!
Souviens-toi du poète! enfant, une prière
Pour chacun des baisers que tu reçus de nous!

décembre 1840

A M. Hilarion Huc[a]

Quand l'an passé, parrain de la *Chronique,*
La couronnant de poétiques fleurs,
Barde inspiré de notre république,
Du vieux Taylor j'arborai les couleurs;
Quand je prédis que les Etats en masse
Eliraient tous le nouveau Washington,
En ricanant tu fis une grimace:
Huc, mon cher Huc, suis-je prophète ou non?

Ignorais-tu qu'en tout temps les poètes,
De l'avenir perçant l'obscurité,
Depuis les jours des bibliques prophètes,
Ont éclairé l'aveugle humanité?
Ignorais-tu?... mais, plaignant ma folie,
Tu me jugeais digne d'un cabanon.
Ah! pour *old Zach* le Nord au Sud s'allie:
Huc, mon cher Huc, suis-je prophète ou non?

Old Zach! ce nom partout dans la mêlée
Retentissait; d'héroïques conscrits,
Sous l'étendard, à la moire étoilée,
Le saluaient de *hourras* et de cris.

174

As, like a frail bud on a rose, you lay
Asleep upon love's bosom, chastely fair.

Now, even more I envy you; for, in
His vast, mysterious wealth of kindliness,
God freed you from life's exile, pent therein:
On earth I envied you; in heaven, no less!

Think of your mother, of your family—
And, thankless not, think of the poet too!—
Weeping, calling your name, on bended knee:
A prayer, child, for each kiss we gave to you!

December 1840

---

a. From "Ecrits sur le tombeau" in *Les Rayons et les ombres*.

For Monsieur Hilarion Huc[a]

When, last year, in the *Chronique,* piously
I played our nation's bard inspired, and sported
Old Taylor's[b] colors, and, with poetry,
Heaped flowers upon him and his cause supported;
When I predicted that the States would all
Elect to power this Washington *nouveau,*
You grimaced with a sneering caterwaul:
Am I, dear Huc, a prophet? Yes or no?

What? Know you not that, since the Bible's day,
The poet-seer is a prophetic being,
Whose gaze pierces the darkness, lights the way,
From year to year, for Mankind's eyes unseeing?
You pitied me, thought my mind lost its tether,
Said I was mad, fit for a cell! But oh!
For *Old Zack,* North and South now come together!
Am I, dear Huc, a prophet? Yes or no?

Old Zack! By shimmering star-strewn flag, brave men,
Everywhere in the midst of war's éclat,
Would hear that name and, over and again,
Greet it with cheers, and shout a loud *huzzah.*

Ce nom seul est un gage de victoire,
En temps de paix comme au feu du canon;
Ce nom jamais n'a triomphé sans gloire:
Huc, mon cher Huc, suis-je prophète ou non?

Zach! le plus beau des grands noms populaires!
Nom immortel adoré des soldats!
Soldats de ligne et soldats volontaires
Le répétaient au milieu des combats.
Un peuple entier aujourd'hui le répète,
Du Maryland au lointain Orégon:
Taylor jamais n'essuya de défaite:
Huc, mon cher Huc, suis-je prophète ou non?

Oui, l'Amérique a choisi le plus digne;
Ce noble exemple à la France est offert:
La Présidence est un honneur insigne
Que le génie ou la gloire conquiert.
L'orage affreux qui te bat, pauvre France,
Vaisseau brisé, démâté, sans timon,
Hélas! hélas!... c'est ta propre inconstance !...
Pour la France, Huc, suis-je prophète?... Non!

janvier 1849

———

a. The poem was set to the tune of "T'en souviens-tu,
    disait un Capitaine."

Le Célibataire[a]

A M. A. V.

Pour s'amuser, boire ici-bas,
Cher Albert, il faut être libre,
Il faut n'avoir point sur les bras
De femme à la langue qui vibre:
Oh! quand on rentre à la maison,
Une moitié crie et s'exclame,

That name: victory's glorious guarantor,
By cannon's roar and, in peace, no less so;
That name, whose every triumph shines the more:
Am I, dear Huc, a prophet? Yes or no?

Zack! Of all names most beautiful, undying,
Beloved by soldiers of each rank and station:
Behind the lines, in combat death-defying,
Everywhere... And today, throughout the nation,
One and all still repeat it, far and near,
From Maryland to Oregon!... For, lo!
Defeat has never marred Taylor's career:
Am I, dear Huc, a prophet? Yes or no?

Ah, yes! America chooses the best,
Most noble: fine example for you, France!
The Presidency is the worthiest
Honor that talent and proud circumstance
Bestow!... Poor France!—Ship mastless, rudderless—
Alas! Alack! You waver to and fro,
Victim of your aimless capriciousness!...
For France am I a prophet, Huc?... Ah, no!

January 1849

---

a. We were unable to identify Hilarion Huc.
b. Zachary Taylor (1784-1850) became the twelfth president of the
   United States in 1849. *La Chronique* (1847-49) was a weekly politi-
   cal and literary journal. It was purchased in 1849 by Charles Testut
   (see p. 198), who attempted to expand circulation by including a
   literary supplement that published many Creole poets.

The Bachelor[a]

For M. A. V.

To drink and revel here below,
Albert, dear friend, one must be free;
One's arms must not be filled—oh no!—
With wife whose tongue flaps endlessly.
When home one comes, a wife will shout
And clamor to a fare-thee-well,

A vous ôter toute raison,
A vous faire damner votre âme.

L'homme seul qui reste garçon
Est heureux, libre sur la terre;
Seul il peut vivre à sa façon:
Ah! sois toujours célibataire.

Le célibat, selon Bonnard,
Est le seul état délectable;
Un garçon peut rentrer fort tard,
Ou bien découcher... sous la table:
Dans les cafés, estaminets,
Il peut fumer cigare ou pipe,
Vider sa bourse et ses goussets.
Sans craindre au retour de Xantippe.

L'homme seul qui reste garçon
Est heureux, libre sur la terre:
Seul il peut vivre à sa façon:
Ah! sois toujours célibataire.

O célibat! la liberté,
Le bonheur toujours t'accompagne;
Oui, le célibat de gaîté
S'enivre ainsi que de champagne:
Le garçon est partout fêté,
La femme esclave à ses pieds tombe:
L'époux, de tout déshérité,
Est comme scellé dans la tombe.

L'homme seul qui reste garçon
Est heureux, libre sur la terre;
Seul il peut vivre à sa façon:
Ah! sois toujours célibataire.

Si d'hymen vous portez le joug,
Vous êtes perdu sans ressource;
On mettra le scellé sur tout,
Sur votre cœur, sur votre bourse;

Until she wears your reason out
And makes you damn your soul to hell.

He who remains unwifed is ever
Happy and free in this our life:
Free to do what he will—whatever!
Never! Ah, never take a wife!

The wifeless life, Bonnard[b] has said,
Is best; for man unwed is able
To stay out late, or shun his bed
And go to sleep... under the table!
In coffee-house and tavern, he
May smoke cigars and pipes galore,
Pour out his gold unstintingly,
Nor fear Xanthippe[c] at his door!

He who remains unwifed is ever
Happy and free in this our life:
Free to do what he will—whatever!
Never! Ah, never take a wife!

O single life! Freedom unbounded:
Happiness follows in your train;
Single life, by delights surrounded,
Drunken on joy, like fine champagne.
Everywhere is the bachelor feted:
Woman falls at his feet; but doom
Attends the spouse, domesticated,
Laid low, like corpse sealed in the tomb.

He who remains unwifed is ever
Happy and free in this our life:
Free to do what he will—whatever!
Never! Ah, never take a wife!

If you the yoke of marriage bear,
Resourceless will you live; and, worse,
You will be pestered everywhere,
Dispossessed of both heart and purse;

Vous êtes comme un animal
Domestique ou bête de somme:
D'après le code conjugal,
A la femme appartient son homme.

L'homme seul qui reste garçon
Est heureux, libre sur la terre:
Seul il peut vivre à sa façon:
Ah! sois toujours célibataire.

Le diable, lorsqu'il devint vieux,
Se convertit, se fit ermite;
C'est un parti sage et pieux
Que plus d'un vieux garçon imite;
Oui, garçon, la meilleure part
T'attend en ce monde et dans l'autre:
C'est ce que dit le vieux Bonnard,
Ce que dit Paul, le grand apôtre!

L'homme seul qui reste garçon
Est heureux, libre sur la terre;
Seul il peut vivre à sa façon:
Ah! sois toujours célibataire.

1849

---

a. The poem was set to the tune of "Roland."

A un Vieillard Débauché

Vieillard, aux blancs cheveux, ému d'un saint respect,
Quand tu passes, tout front s'incline à ton aspect:
La Nouvelle-Orléans, comme Lacédémone,
Aime un front où du temps la majesté rayonne:
Environné d'égards et d'amour entouré,
Pour nous, comme la femme, un vieillard est sacré...
Mais souvent le vieillard, qui doit à tous l'exemple

An animal are you, monsieur,
Like madame's pet or packload cattle.
So says the marriage code: for her,
The husband is but common chattel.

He who remains unwifed is ever
Happy and free in this our life:
Free to do what he will—whatever!
Never! Ah, never take a wife!

The devil, growing long of tooth,
As an ascetic chose to dwell:
A wise and pious choice, forsooth,
That many old bachelors make as well;
Yes, unwed friend, the best awaits
In this world and the next withal:
At least our old Bonnard so states;
So, too, the great apostle Paul!

He who remains unwifed is ever
Happy and free in this our life:
Free to do what he will—whatever!
Never! Ah, never take a wife!

   1849

----

a. We were unable to identify "A. V."
b. This may be a reference to le chevalier Bernard
   de Bonnard (1740–74), a minor poet.
c. Xanthippe was Socrates' wife. She was said to have
   had a bad temper and is the personification of the
   nagging wife.

For a Dissolute Old Man

Old man, of holy mien and hair of white,
When you pass by, all heads bow at your sight;
New Orleans, like brave Sparta's noble clime,
Loves a brow where time's majesty sublime
Shines forth: surrounded by solicitude
And loving kindness, an old man is viewed—
Like woman—as a sacred being. And yet,

Des plus hautes vertus, comme le prêtre au temple,
Des saintes lois de Dieu follement affranchi,
Le vieillard n'est souvent *qu'un sépulcre blanchi:*
Oui, quand d'un peuple entier le respect le protège,
Il n'est qu'un vil fumier que recouvre la neige.

Nouvelle-Orléans, juin 1856

A M. * * *

Vieillard qui, de ton or ne pleurant pas la perte,
Vis seul et satisfait comme le vieux Laërte,
Toi qui fus comme Job par le Seigneur frappé,
Sans qu'un murmure soit de ton cœur échappé,
Sans que jamais ta voix ait accusé personne,
Sans avoir maudit Dieu qui reprend ce qu'il donne;
Héroïque chrétien, qui de la pauvreté
As compris la grandeur, la joie et la beauté;
Vieux colon qui, semblable au vieillard de Virgile,
Maître d'un petit champ que ta main rend fertile,
Dans l'amour du travail as trouvé le bonheur;
O saint vieillard *ayant tout perdu fors l'honneur!*
Ah! que j'aime, fuyant loin de la multitude,
A visiter parfois ton humble solitude,
A te voir ferme et droit, comme un pin foudroyé,
Meurtri par l'ouragan, mais sans être ployé,
Et qui, dans la forêt couverte de ruines,
Plonge orgueilleusement ses profondes racines!

juillet 1856

Often, the old man, who ought not forget
That he, like temple priest, should be the very
Model of highest virtues exemplary,
Casts off God's laws and, as the Pharisee,
Naught but a *whited sepulcher* is he!
Yes, though by one and all he stands respected,
He is a dungheap vile, by snow protected.

New Orleans, June 1856

For Monsieur * * *

Old man, bereft of gold, yet weeping not,
Content like old Laertes with your lot;
Living alone and, like Job, whom the Lord
Afflicted: yet you hurl no curses toward
Your God, who gives and takes away, nor mutter
The slightest rancor of your heart, nor utter
The merest lamentation of your woe;
Heroic Christian, you who, saintly, know
Poverty's grandeur, joy, and beauty; you,
Old planter, who like Virgil's elder,[a] do
Honor to your most modest plot of land,
Render it fertile with an honest hand,
And who find happiness in laboring;
Holy old man, you who *lost everything*
Save honor! Ah! How I enjoy—delight—
Fleeing the multitude and, in my flight,
Visiting you in humble solitude;
Seeing you, like the pine—straight, unsubdued
Despite the lightning and the hurricane—
The pine that strong and solid will remain,
And that, in woods laid waste on every side,
Plunges yet deep its roots with stalwart pride!

July 1856

---

a. A reference to Virgil's *Georgics* 4.116–48

A M * * *

Pour celui qui n'a plus ici-bas une mère,
La vie est un exil et la gloire est amère.

Hélas! sans une mère, au sourire divin,
Une couronne pèse au front de l'orphelin;
Non, ne me parlez plus de lauriers et de gloire:
La gloire n'est qu'un mot, et je n'y veux plus croire:
Soumet, barde divin, de la France l'orgueil,
Soumet l'a dit: *La gloire est un manteau de deuil.*

Pour celui qui n'a plus ici-bas une mère.
La vie est un exil, et la gloire est amère.

octobre 1856

For M * * *

For him bereft of mother here below,
Life is an exile; glory, a bitter woe.

No mother with her heavenly smile! Ah me!
The orphan's richest crown weighs heavily
Upon his brow! Speak not of laurels' glory:
Vain words, these; naught but empty allegory!
Divine Soumet[a]—bard, pride of France—has said:
Glory is but a cloak to mourn the dead.

For him bereft of mother here below,
Life is an exile; glory, a bitter woe.

October 1856

---

a. Alexandre Soumet (1788–1845) was a much-admired
   French playwright and poet whose collections of poetry
   include *Jeanne d'Arc* (1846).

Le Louisianais

La valeur est pour lui la moindre des vertus;
Il est grand, généreux: son âme haute et fière
Peut servir de proverbe aux peuples de la terre.
Avec cet apanage, il est doté de plus

Tullius Saint-Céran (1800–1855)

Tullius Saint-Céran was born of French parents on Jamaica in 1800. An insurrection drove the family from the island, and in 1805 they moved to New Orleans, where Saint-Céran grew up. At nineteen Saint-Céran learned the printer's trade, and when he failed to make his fortune in Cuba, he returned to New Orleans. He then married Anna Livingston, cousin to Edouard Livingston, a state senator and later secretary of state. In 1825 Saint-Céran became the editor of the French section of *Gazette de la Louisiane,* in whose pages, underscoring his republican sentiments, he dropped the aristocratic particle from his name, Tullius de Saint-Céran. Gifted in languages, Saint-Céran wrote fluently in Spanish and English and made his living translating and teaching modern languages. The first part of his autobiographical novel, *The Adventures of Marius,* was published in English.

Saint-Céran's first volume of poetry, *Chansons et poésies diverses,* made up of poems published in *L'Abeille,* appeared in 1836. His second volume, pretentiously entitled *Rien—ou moi! Poésies nouvelles,* appeared in 1837. *Rien—ou moi!* (myself or nothing at all) connotes the romantic idea that the self, and particularly the poet, is the only authentic source of goodness, truth, and beauty. In 1838 Saint-Céran published *Mil huit cent quatorze et mil huit cent quinze ou les combats et la victoire des fils de la Louisiane* (1814 and 1815; or, the battle and victory of the sons of Louisiana), an epic poem on the Battle of New Orleans. Saint-Céran's last publication, *Les Louisianaises,* appeared in 1840. He died in New Orleans in 1855. The poems included here are from *Rien—ou moi!* The vigor and bravado of Saint-Céran's poetry are illustrated in "The Louisianan" and "Woe unto Him Who Wrongs Me." His generation's veneration of the popular French romantic poet Pierre-Jean de Béranger is succinctly conveyed in the couplet "Béranger."

The Louisianan

Lofty is he, man great and generous;
For him, the least of virtues is one's worth:
Noble-souled model, he, for all the earth.
And, with those gifts displayed, he shows to us

D'un jugement profond, d'un esprit saisissant
Qui remplacent pour lui les leçons du collége.
Il peut s'enorgueillir surtout du privilège
De trancher par l'éclat d'un don plus ravissant:

Un talisman vivant! un plus brillant joyau
Que ceux que l'on découvre aux mains du lapidaire:
L'IMAGINATION, cette magique pierre
Qui fait souvent pâlir le lumineux flambeau

Du savoir. Il possède encor d'autres trésors;
Son physique répond aux GRANDS TRAITS de son âme:
Son œil est un miroir que le soleil enflamme,
Et le cèdre peut seul vous simuler son corps!

Sur la Mort d'un Ami

Imitation

"De ses ailes," sur toi, "déployant l'envergure,"
La Mort, de tes beaux jours éteignit le flambeau,
Et saisit tout d'un coup son immense pâture,
Pour l'aller dévorer dans la nuit du tombeau!

En la muerte de un amigo

Excerpt

Tendió la Muerte sus horrendas alas;
Como buitre voraz cayó en mi amigo;
Y en él, sus garras con furor clavando,
A la honda huesa le arrastró consigo.

(Manuel José Quintana, from "En la muerte de
un amigo")

Béranger

De tout tems, des chansons l'essaim fut importun:
Mais des grands chansonniers dites-moi le nombre: un!

A depth of judgment and a vigorous mind,
More worthy, far, than lessons learned in class;
Proud of the favor, when choice comes to pass,
To use that brightest gift that one can find—

And with éclat!—a living charm, gem rare,
More brilliant than fine jeweler's hands have known:
To wit, IMAGINATION!... Magic stone
That, ofttimes, makes to pale, beyond compare,

Knowledge's torch... Still other treasures, his
As well: his eye's glance mirrors the sun's flame;
And his soul's VIRTUES echo in his frame,
Stalwart, tall, as naught but the cedar is!

On the Death of a Friend

Imitation[a]

Death snuffed the torch, with wings unfurled, outspread—
The torch that shed upon your youth its light—
Then clawed his prey and, eager to be fed,
Went to devour it in the tomb's deep night!

---

a. This "imitation" is based on the last four lines of "En la muerte de
un amigo" (1802), by Manuel José Quintana (1772–1857), a Spanish
poet and liberal born in Madrid and best known for patriotic odes
such as *El Panteón del Escorial* (1805).

Béranger

Ever have songs swarmed, vexed us, never done:
But count for me the great song-poets: one!

Sur un Petit Enfant

Couvert d'un Parapluie

Cher enfant, que ne peut ta jeune âme, qu'épie
Déjà ce noir autour que l'on nomme le Sort,
Trouver, comme ton front, un port contre la vie!
Un jour tu connaîtras le malheur et la mort!

Malheur à Qui M'Outrage!

Malheur à qui m'outrage, et que la retenue
M'empêche d'assaillir dans ma colère nue!
Car mon cœur garde tout: ce n'est point l'océan,
Où s'efface bientôt le choc de l'ouragan;
C'est le rocher tronqué par la foudre, et qui porte
Sa blessure toujours, comme lui-même, forte!

On a Little Child

Beneath an Umbrella

Dear child, would that your young soul—spied here, now,
By that black hawk called Fate—might find the way
To safety from life's shoals, as does your brow!
Ah! But you will know woe and death one day!

Woe unto Him Who Wrongs Me

Woe unto him who wrongs me, and whom naught
But my restraint saves from my wrath, distraught!
My heart yields nothing up: not like the ocean,
Where quickly vanishes the storm's commotion;
It is the rocky cliff, by lightning split,
Ever bearing its wound, but strong, like it!

Couplet[a]

Contre une demoiselle sur qui
on avait tiré un coup de pistolet

Avec plus de timidité,
De douceur dans le caractère,
Et le regard moins effronté,
Peut-être Elina pourrait plaire:
Mais loin d'avoir les dons heureux
Qui font rechercher une belle,
Elina n'allume des feux—
Que pour lui brûler la cervelle.

————

a. This poem was set to the tune of "Femmes,
   voulez-vous éprouver."

Michel St. Pierre (1810–52)

A Creole of color, Michel St. Pierre was born in 1810 into a devout
Catholic family of New Orleans. St. Pierre's father made sure that
his children were pious and well educated. Michel St. Pierre made his living
as a fencing master and was nicknamed the "Creole Bayard."[1] By 1846, how-
ever, he had opened a school for children of both sexes. Virtually all St. Pierre's
poetry was published in *Les Cenelles*. In "Two Years Later" he thanks Auguste
Populus for coming to his aid when he had contemplated suicide. (Populus's
"Reply" is included in this volume.) And "Lines" is surely one of the most
surprising poems in the romantic vein. Pierre St. Michel died in 1852. His fu-
neral oration was composed and delivered by Armand Lanusse and then pub-
lished in *L'Abeille*.

---

1. Pierre du Terrail (1475–1525), known as le Chevalier Bayard, was a legendary soldier. In a
   remarkable career that spanned three decades, Bayard fought under Charles VIII and was
   commended by François I. Ferocious in battle, Bayard was also revered as the ideal man of
   honor.

Lines

Concerning a young lady
who had been shot at

Perchance, were Elina more shy,
And of a mien and manner sweeter,
Were she less arrogant of eye,
One might, I think, be pleased to meet her.
But never will man persevere
To seek her beauty round about:
Elina sparks no fires, I fear—
Except to have her brains blown out.

A une Demoiselle

qui me demandait des vers pour son album

Belle enfant que l'Amour a pris soin de parer
De ses plus beaux attraits pour mieux nous inspirer;
Que puis-je vous offrir dans ma mélancolie?
Depuis long-temps mon cœur est las de poésie,
Et malgré le désir que j'éprouve en ce jour
De chanter l'innocence et de plaire à l'amour,
Je crains bien que ma voix, hélas! trop langoureuse,
Ne vous fasse pleurer—quand vous êtes heureuse!
Heureuse! soyez-le. Que du ciel la faveur
Maintienne près de vous la paix et le bonheur,
Vous préserve des maux dont la vie est semée,
Et vous la rende enfin joyeuse et parfumée!

Deux ans après

A mon ami A. Populus

Ami, si l'espérance habite encor mon cœur,
Si parfois je souris et parle de bonheur,
Si l'avenir me plaît dans ma nouvelle vie,
Je le dois à toi seul—et je t'en remercie!
Sans toi le désespoir allait briser mes jours,
J'étais près du tombeau.—Tu vins à mon secours!—
Tu ne délaissas point l'ami de ton enfance,
Tu lui tendis la main.—Il en a souvenance!—
Ton aspect ranima son courage abattu.—
Contre le cruel sort tu soutins sa vertu.—
Aujourd'hui je viens donc, quittant ma solitude,
T'exprimer de mon cœur toute la gratitude;
La vérité m'inspire et son divin flambeau
Fait briller à mes yeux son éclat le plus beau!—
Je le redis encor, dans ma douleur profonde
Je voulais pour toujours renoncer à ce monde,
Lorsque tu rappelas mon esprit égaré,
Me fis voir mon erreur qu'à ta voix j'abjurai.
L'amitié donne à l'âme une toute puissance

For a Young Lady

who asked me for a poem as a keepsake

Beautiful child, on whom Love carefully
Bestowed his charms—his fairest—so that we
Might be inspired, what can I offer you
In my deep melancholy? Once, I knew
Poetry's joys, but now, long since do I
Grow tired of it; and, though I would comply
To please your love and sing your innocence,
I fear my voice languishes, sad; and, hence,
Well might you weep despite your happiness!
And so be happy! May you long possess
Heaven's peaceful cheer, safe from life's woes, contented,
With days all pleasure-filled and fragrant-scented.

Two Years Later

For my friend A. Populus

My friend, if hope dwells in my heart again,
If I smile and sound happy now and then,
If my new life, my future, pleases me,
I owe it all to you—and earnestly
I thank you! For, without you, my despair
Threatened to dash my days. I hovered there,
About the grave... But you never forgot
Your childhood friend... Now he forgets you not,
You who came to his aid in dark duress,
Held out your hand... With your mere presence, yes,
You brought him back to life, you succored him,
And gave him strength against fate's ruthless whim.
So too I come today, leaving behind
My solitude, hoping my heart can find
Words for its thanks; the truth's divine torch fires
Before my gaze its loveliest flames, inspires
My soul and mind! Again do I repeat
That when, in my deep woe, I would retreat
Ever from this life, you it was who brought

De vaincre le malheur, de calmer la souffrance;
C'est un ange envoyé du céleste séjour
Pour nous entretenir d'espérance et d'amour.

My errant spirit back, and whose voice taught
The folly of my ways; if I recanted,
Friendship it was—as ever it is—that granted
My soul the boon omnipotent to bring
Distress to heel, and offer solacing:
Friendship, that angel sent from heaven above
To proffer us words filled with hope and love.

Charles Testut (ca. 1819–92)

Charles Testut, a French émigré who came to the United States in 1839, was probably born in 1819. Although Testut would later practice homeopathic medicine, he was one of the most prolific writers of the period. In 1843 he went to Guadeloupe with his wife and son just in time for an earthquake that devastated the island; the family survived but returned to New Orleans penniless. In the following years Testut worked as a journalist and in time managed to start a paper in Alabama, although it later failed. He returned to New Orleans, where he bought another paper that also failed, whereupon he moved to yet another newspaper; it became a way of life. Everything Charles Testut wrote, whether journalism, poetry, fiction, or nonfiction, expressed the volatile period in which he lived. In the poem "Le Poète," dedicated to the poet and Creole of color Camille Thierry, Testut states explicitly that the poet is the moral and spiritual conscience of a society. For Testut, the poet's role was more important than that of the politician or captain of industry. Charles Testut's first book of poetry, *Les Echos*, was published in 1849; this was followed in 1851 by *Fleurs d'été*. By 1858 he had completed *Vieux Solomon*, an abolitionist novel that was not published until 1872. Testut and his family were in New York City in 1858, but by 1871 he was back in New Orleans, where he became editor of the journal *L'Equité*. During that turbulent and racially explosive period, Testut stated that *L'Equité* was dedicated to the reconciliation of the races and universal progress. Unfortunately, Testut's critique of Pope Pius IX, support of freemasonry, and advocacy of the black cause quickly put the paper out of business. Among the Frenchmen who were willing to work with Creoles of color, Testut became a correspondent for the first black daily newspaper, *La Tribune*, in 1865.

A M. Alex. Latil

Rien!—Résigné, j'attends qu'ému de ma souffrance,
Dieu sur moi fasse luire un rayon d'espérance,
Ou que, dans sa bonté
Du malheur qui m'opprime il brise le calice,
Et termine bientôt ma vie et mon supplice,
En m'appelant au sein de son éternité!

—Alex. Latil

Charles Testut's contributions to the definition and development of Louisiana's literature were exceptional. In 1849 he published *Les Veillées louisianaises* (Louisiana evenings), which comprised two volumes of historical novels set in Louisiana, including works by Testut, Armand Garreau, and Hégésippe Moreau. In 1850 he published *Portraits littéraires de la Nouvelle-Orléans,* a collection of brief essays on approximately forty Louisiana writers including the Creoles of color Armand Lanusse, Camille Thierry, and Joanni Questy. In 1852 Testut attended his first séance and soon after was converted, like a number of his peers, to spiritualism. The spirits with whom Testut and others such as Joanni Questy and Adolphe Duhart convened were especially supportive of these romantic writers' radical political goals, such as the abolition of slavery, racial equality, and a truly democratic republic. In 1854 Testut published a collection of spiritual "communications," *Manifestations spirituelles.* He spent the last years of his life in poverty and died in New Orleans in 1892. The poetry included here comes from *Les Echos* and *Fleurs d'été.* Imbued with a romantic sensibility, the poems "For Monsieur Alex. Latil" and "On the Death of the Author of *Les Ephémères*" commemorate the Louisiana poet Alexandre Latil (see p. 99). The encomium "Washington" celebrates the "father of the country," just as "The Poor Man's Funeral Procession" honors the passing of a nameless pauper.

All the following poems come from *Les Echos,* except "On the Death of the Author of *Les Ephémères*" and "The Poor Man's Funeral Procession," which come from *Fleurs d'été.*

For Monsieur Alex. Latil

> Nothing! Resigned, I wait in agony
> For God to shine a ray of hope on me,
>   Or, by His kindness blessed,
> To see Him smash my cup, with woe full rife,
> And end this punishment that is my life,
> Calling me to His bosom's endless rest!
>
> —Alexandre Latil[a]

Pauvre enfant du malheur, oh! que ton chant est triste;
Que ta plainte est touchante et doit monter vers Dieu,
Quand tu jettes en tes vers, poétique psalmiste,
  Et ta souffrance et ton adieu!

Car elle fut pour toi bien dure et bien amère
La coupe de la vie! et tu n'as pas longtems
Bercé ton avenir de la douce chimère
  Qui donne au cœur de si doux chants!

Oh! de tes vers en pleurs que je sens l'harmonie...
Oh! comme ta souffrance arrive et chante en moi...
C'est, sur sa harpe d'or, la plaintive Ionie
  Qui nous jette un lugubre émoi.

Poète des douleurs, qu'une douce croyance,
Comme un baume divin, dore ton avenir!
Si tu souffres ici-bas, va! crois en l'Espérance:
  Rien ici-bas ne doit finir.

Puisque chacun de nous traîne, sur cette terre,
Une croix de douleur toujours lourde à porter,
Regardons, par-delà notre triste hémisphère,
  Le ciel où nous devons monter!

Déjà, pour alléger ton horrible souffrance,
A tes cris de détresse un ange est descendu;
Ah! que sa voix, pour toi, soit la douce espérance
  Du bien qui te sera rendu!

Aux soins de chaque jour que sa main te prodigue,
Même au fort de tes maux, ne reconnais-tu pas
Que la main du Seigneur soulageant ta fatigue,
  Jette un espoir devant tes pas?...

Courage, oh mon poète! à cette triste vie
Nous devons tous un jour dire un dernier adieu:
Celui qui souffrira sans haine et sans envie,
  Ira se reposer en Dieu!

Poor child of woe! How sad that song of yours!
To God himself how your lament must rise,
When, in your psalms, your soulful spirit pours
    Your anguishings and your goodbyes!

For life's cup offered you its bitterest brew!
And all too short a time did destiny
Hold out those tender, lulling dreams to you
    That let a heart sing joyously!

Oh! Sadly sweet, your weeping "welladays,"
That sound your verse sings in me, dolorous...
Plaintive Ionian harp of gold, it lays
    Its drear and mournful pall on us.

Poet of pain, may faith's glow gild your grief
Like a divine balm, gently spread thereon!
Today you pine... Ah! Let Hope bring relief:
    Tomorrow will live on and on.

Since each of us, in this life here below,
Must torment's heavy cross forever bear,
Let us look past this dour world's vale of woe
    To heaven, whither we shall repair.

Already, hearing your sighs of distress,
An angel fair descends to soothe your pain;
Ah! May his voice foretell with tenderness
    That boon soon to be yours again!

From each day's torment may He grant surcease!
What? See you not the Lord's hand there, beside you,
Though deep your bale and bane, to bring you peace,
    Casting a ray of hope to guide you?

Courage, dear poet! To life's misery
We all, one day, must say a last farewell:
And he who suffers calmly, rancor-free,
    With sweet repose in God shall dwell!

———————

a. Alexandre Latil's "Amour et Douleur" is the fourth éphémère.

Washington

Ton nom, c'est l'avenir; ton nom, c'est le grand phare
Que tout peuple opprimé regarde en tressaillant...
C'est le chant éternel! c'est l'ardente fanfare;
C'est le cri du désert que jette le Tartare,
    Quand son coursier bondit, fuyant!

Washington! Washington! Partout l'écho sonore,
Au tocsin de ton nom, répète: Libèrté!
Des rives du Couchant aux rives de l'Aurore,
Tout tuRan te maudit, mais tout peuple t'adore...
    Tout homme libre t'a chanté!

Depuis que, d'un regard, Dieu fit surgir le monde,
Pour ses desseins sacrés, nul n'a mieux combattu;
Nul n'a, dans l'avenir, de trace plus profonde;
Sur les champs éternels, une loi plus féconde:
    La Liberté, c'est la Vertu!

A peine es-tu parti... déjà partout résonne
Un chant d'indépendance, allant vers l'avenir!
Les tyrans ont pâli!... partout le tocsin sonne;
Le glaive ardent s'abat sur les fronts à couronne...
    Déjà déjà voici venir,

Voici venir enfin, dans la foudre qui gronde,
Voici venir le jour si long-tems attendu!
Partout germe et grandit, dans la terre profonde,
Le grain que tu jetas à la sève féconde
    Du sang noblement répandu!

Il roulera sans fin sur l'océan des âges
Ton vaisseau glorieux... sans redouter les vents...
L'étendard populaire, un jour, sur tous rivages
Flottera radieux, après bien des orages,
    Calme, au milieu des flots mouvants!

Washington

Your name bespeaks the future: beacon light
Gazed on by earth's oppressed, trembling their need;
A timeless hymn; a fanfare burning bright;
The cry of desert Tartar taking flight,
    Bounding upon his leaping steed!

Washington! Washington! With one accord,
From West to East the echoing shores proclaim:
Liberty! By the tyrant cursed, abhorred,
But by the people worshiped and adored...
    All free men glorify your name!

Since God glanced this, our world, to life from naught,
For His eternal ends there has been none
Who has more deeply sown the future, wrought
His law more fertile, with fierce combat bought:
    Virtue and liberty are one!

Scarce are you gone... Already, future-bound,
The song of independence rings! Pale grow
The tyrants roundabout!... The tocsins sound;
The fiery sword smites down heads haughty-crowned...
    Already now... Already, oh!...

Lo! Comes the long-awaited day at last,
Howling with thunder, growling, tempest-fed!
Everywhere sprouts to life, amid the blast,
Deep in the earth, the fertile seed you cast,
    Nourished by blood so nobly shed!

Ever your glorious craft will sail time's sea,
Fearless, despite the gale... One day, with pride,
On every shore, flags of a people free,
After the storm, will billow tranquilly
    Above the rising, swelling tide!

Déjà nous entendons cet hosanna sublime
Que cent millions de voix entonneront en chœur,
Quand, de la tyrannie comblant le vaste abîme,
Le monde aura pleuré sa dernière victime,
        Brisé son dernier oppresseur!

Il ne te fallut pas la pourpre tyrannique,
Les licteurs et la hache et l'orgueil des Césars:
Cincinnatus plus grand, ton sceptre despotique
C'était la liberté! c'était la République
        Qui courbera le front des Czars!

Est-il un plus grand jour aux pages de l'histoire.
Ils étaient là... debout et le front découvert,
Calmes, dignes et forts d'une sublime gloire:
Du vil joug d'Albion ils chassent la mémoire...
        Ecoutez!... quel noble concert:

"A la face du ciel... de Dieu qui nous écoute,
"Soyons libres demain! et libres pour toujours!
"Hommes, entre la honte et la mort, plus de doute...
"Que l'Anglais insolent reprenne enfin sa route,
        "Ou que son corps reste aux vautours."

Ils ont dit.—Et l'écho, chargé de leur parole,
A partout répondu: Liberté! Liberté...
La lutte a commencé, sans trêve, ardente et folle...
Le Léopard a fui... l'Aigle triomphe!... il vole
        Dans ses airs, avec majesté!

A toi, gloire à jamais, Père de la Patrie!
Ton grand nom grandira toujours dans l'avenir...
Le jour que règnera la Liberté chérie,
Un chant s'élèvera de toute âme attendrie:
        Chant de gloire à ton souvenir!

Soon hear we that hosanna! Voices massed
Sublime, a hundred million raised as one,
When—tyranny's fell reign, forever past,
And full its foul abyss, its chasm vast—
    Man's last oppressor lies undone!

You needed not the tyrant's purple, nor
The lictor's axe, the Caesars' posturings;
Like Cincinnatus, firm the power you bore:
Liberty! The Republic! Nothing more
    To bow the heads of czars and kings!

Do history's pages boast a finer day?
There they stood, brows bare, staunchly calm their spirit...
And, with the noisome memory cast away—
Albion's vile yoke!—ready for the fray!
    Ah! Noble concert!... Listen! Hear it!...

"Before God, giving ear from heaven's height:
Freedom tomorrow! Always!... He ordains
Death before shame—more pleasing in His sight!
Let haughty English foe at last take flight,
    Or leave the buzzards his remains!"

So they spoke. And the echoes, everywhere,
Full of their weighty words, cried: "Liberty!..."
Long raged the battle, fierce its blast and blare...
The Leopard[a] fled... The Eagle took the air,
    Majestic in its victory!

O Father of the Country, haloed be!
Your great name will grow greater still for us...
The day when liberty reigns peacefully
A hymn will rise from all humanity
    And bless your memory glorious!

---

a. Clearly a personification of the British, albeit an unusual one.

Adieu

Pourtant hélas! vous m'aviez dit: je t'aime!
Et maintenant votre amour a passé,
Et je vous quitte à cette place même
Où le bonheur pour nous a commencé!
Quand vous cherchiez un aveu dans mes larmes,
Vous me disiez: voilà mon plus beau jour!
Et maintenant, sous un ciel sans alarmes,
Vous êtes las déjà de mon amour!

En vous quittant, je ne serai pas fière
Pour vous cacher la peine de mon cœur;
Un jour viendra que cette heure dernière
Sera pour vous une amère douleur...
Je serai loin et, dans votre pensée,
Mon souvenir peut-être habitera,
Quand le repos, à votre âme blessée,
Comme un regret, du passé parlera.

Adieu! je pars... vous, dans les bruits du monde,
Allez noyer l'importun souvenir
De ces longs jours pleins d'une paix profonde
Que je rêvais pour un long avenir...
Bonheur, amour, soins, amitié, tendresse,
Oubliez tout au bruit de gais ébats:
Moi, seule hélas! seule avec ma tristesse,
Je puis mourir, mais je n'oublîrai pas!

Adieu! je pleure... adieu! bientôt peut-être
Serez-vous las de tous ces vains plaisirs,
Et du bonheur l'image fera naître
D'un doux passé le rêve et les désirs...
Moi, j'attendrai, bien triste mais constante,
Chaque matin, guettant votre retour:
Pauvre blessé, revenez sous ma tente
Vous reposer auprès de mon amour!

Farewell[a]

Alas! You said: "I love you!" And yet, how
Can it be that your love is ended thus?
I leave you in this very place—here, now—
Where happiness first came to life for us!
You said: "This is the fairest day for me!"
When, through my tears, you sought my vow thereof.
And now, beneath a sky spread peacefully,
Monsieur, you tire already of my love!

I shall not be so proud, on losing you,
As to conceal my heart's distress; the day
Will come when this, our final hour's "adieu,"
Will fill you with the bitterest dismay...
Far though I be, perhaps a tender thought
Of me, and of the tranquil time we spent,
Will linger in your soul, memory-wrought,
And speak to you once more of heart's content.

Farewell! I leave you... Go, monsieur! And let
The turmoil of the world drown out the sound
Of a life that I dreamt would long beget
The gentle pleasures of a peace profound...
Happiness, friendship, love, tender affection:
In life's gay whirl, forget them all, the lot!
Alone shall I be, in my sad dejection:
Die though I may, I shall forget them not!

Farewell! I weep... Farewell! Soon you may find
That you grow weary of those pleasures vain,
And that our happy past will call to mind
The dream to live its sweetness once again...
And I, each morning, faithful as before,
Shall scan the sea for your return—east, west...
Poor wounded bird! Beneath my tent, once more,
Come, by my love reposing, take your rest!

---

a. "Farewell" and the following, "The Return," are to be read as
   a pair. "Farewell" is in the woman's voice, and "The Return," in
   that of the man.

Le Retour

Léger navire,
Brise les flots,
Au gai délire
Des matelots...
Je vois la plage
De mon bonheur
Le doux rivage
Cher à mon cœur.

Oh! glisse vite:
Elle m'attend;
Son cœur palpite,
Mon cœur l'entend!
Elle est plus belle
Que les amours;
Voguons vers elle,
Voguons toujours...

Sur la tourelle
Dieu! je la vois;
Mon cœur près d'elle
Vole avant moi!
Sa voix si chère,
Chante aux échos...
Barque légère,
Fendons les flots!

The Return

Barque, plough the waves...
Ah! Land ahoy!
The mates—gay knaves—
Sing loud their joy.
Spread out before
My gaze, I see
The tender shore
Loom lovingly.

Faster!... Draw near!
For she is waiting...
My heart can hear
Hers palpitating.
More beautiful
Than cupids, she!
Pull the oars!... Pull!
Row fast and free...

God! On the tower
I see her, singing...
My heart—O power
Of love!—goes winging
Unto her... Hark!
That voice!... Ah me!...
Fly, gentle barque...
Plough wide the sea!

Sur la Mort de l'Auteur des *Ephémères*

A Madame Veuve A. Latil

Pauvre Latil, adieu! Dans ta couche dernière
Tranquille maintenant ton front s'est endormi...
Tu n'as plus les douleurs, les tourments de la terre,
        Et Dieu, touché de ta prière,
A jeté sur tes maux le pardon d'un ami.

Poëte, tu n'es plus; mais les chants de ta lyre
Vibrent avec tes pleurs dans bien des cœurs émus:
Et lorsque nous songeons aux jours de ton martyre,
        Oh! c'est avec un saint délire
Que nous voyons ta place au milieu des élus!

Tu n'avais pas quitté les bords de ta patrie;
Au doux talent des vers nul ne t'avait formé;
Mais ton âme était d'or, et la muse chérie
        De son plus doux lait l'a nourrie,
Et tu la chérissais comme un fils bien aimé...

Sans elle, pauvre enfant, quelle eût été ta vie,
Puisqu'il était écrit que tu devais souffrir?
Au lieu d'appeler Dieu, par la rage et l'envie
        Ton âme, au ciel bientôt ravie,
Dans des pleurs éternels sans cesse eût dû mourir!

Maintenant qu'à jamais ta souffrance est passée,
Combien ont ici-bas, duré tes mauvais jours?
Tu connais aujourd'hui l'éternelle pensée
        Que, dans notre audace insensée,
Par un doute insultant nous offensons toujours!...

Plus de secrets pour toi! le voile de ce monde
Devant tes yeux ouverts maintenant est baissé;
Ton oreille a reçu la parole profonde...
        Et tu vois la rive féconde
Où le bonheur sourit à la foi du passé!

On the Death of the Author of *Les Ephémères*

For the Widow of the Late A. Latil

Latil, poor soul, farewell! Calm is your brow,
Sleeping, at peace, in final, deep repose.
Finished, for you, life's trials; and, I vow,
    God—much moved by your prayer—has now
Bestowed a friend's redemption on your woes.

Poet, you are no more; but your lyre's strings
Echo your tears in many a tender breast;
And, when we think of all your sufferings,
    Oh, what a saintly joy it brings
To know you, now, among the chosen blessed!

Child of your native land, you never quit
Her soil: your talent formed your verse, homespun.
But golden was your soul, and exquisite
    The muse whose sweet milk nourished it:
She, whom you cherished as a well-loved son.

Poor child! Without her, what dole would have been
Your days, since torment was to be your fate?
Godless, you might have let resentment, sin,
    Pervert your heavenly soul with hate,
And died, endlessly weeping your chagrin!

Now that your anguish is forever past,
How brief, indeed, was your earthly duress!
Today you see God's mind revealed, at last,
    That, with their folly unsurpassed
Some dare to doubt, in their audaciousness!...

No secrets from you now, for all is heard
And seen: before your eyes life's veil is gone;
Unto your ears is given the weighty Word...
    You see that fertile shore, unblurred,
Where your past faith is gently smiled upon!

Aux tourments de nos jours si l'avenir mesure
Les bonheurs à donner à qui n'a pas maudit,
Oh! tu dois être heureux, Latil!... sur ta torture
           Dans un poétique murmure,
Tu chantas... tu pleuras... hélas! et tout fut dit...

Résigné, courageux au milieu du martyre,
Tu ne blasphémais pas, mais demandais à Dieu
Qu'il essuyât bientôt les larmes de ta lyre,
           Lui qui, seul, sait et pourrait dire
Pourquoi l'on souffre tant jusqu'au terrestre adieu!

Patient dans ta foi, croyant comme un poète,
Tu les étonnas bien ceux qui ne savent pas
Que la lyre est un dieu qui, plus bat la tempête,
           Plus il sait couronner la tête
D'éternelle espérance après un vain trépas!

Regarde maintenant, du haut de l'empyrée,
Regarde, enfant du ciel, nos souffrances d'un jour,
Toi qui sais ce que vaut la parole sacrée
           Que du Christ la voix éplorée
Daigna parler à l'homme, objet de son amour...

Quelques instans encore, et ceux que ton cœur aime
Viendront doubler aux cieux ton bonheur éternel;
L'ange qui t'a souri jusqu'à l'heure suprême,
           Bientôt te sourira de même
Dans la sainte oasis où tu jouis, dans le ciel!...

Pauvre Latil, adieu!... Dans ta couche dernière
Tranquille maintenant ton front s'est endormi...
Tu n'as plus les douleurs, les tourments de la terre,
           Et Dieu, touché de ta prière,
A jeté sur tes maux le pardon d'un ami.

If joy is meted out by destiny
To those most cursed, yet who curse not thereat,
Oh! My Latil, how joyous must you be!
  You sighed your pain in poetry:
You sighed... You wept... And that, alas, was that...

Resigned, courageous in your martyrdom,
You blasphemed not, but asked that God might dry
The tears your lyre was shedding, wearisome—
  The good Lord, who, alone, could plumb
Man's pains, endured until life's last goodbye!

With poet's patient faith, you awed all those
Who knew not that the lyre, with sacred breath,
Is a god; that, the more the tempest blows,
  The more it wreathes your head, bestows
Eternal hope after a trivial death!

Look down upon our transient woes—O you,
Now heaven's child—from the empyrean span;
You, who now know the Word, sacred and true,
  That Christ, lamenting, spoke unto
The object of his love eternal: Man...

A moment more, and those you love will then
Double your joy beyond the boundless skies;
The angel who smiled at your last "amen"
  Will smile upon you yet again
In heaven's holy oasis: Paradise!...

Latil, poor soul, farewell! Calm is your brow,
Sleeping at peace, in final, deep repose...
Finished, for you, life's trials; and, I vow,
  God—much moved by your prayer—has now
Bestowed a friend's redemption on your woes.

Le Convoi du Pauvre

A M. Emile Ribereau

Le jour s'éteint, et l'eau tombe glacée;
Le char des morts marche silencieux;
Tout paraît sombre, et la foule pressée
Passe rapide en détournant les yeux...

Quel est celui qui s'en va solitaire,
Dans la charrette aux lugubres couleurs?
Quel est son nom? C'est quelque prolétaire
Dont l'Eternel a fini les douleurs...

Il a passé sans que jamais la foule
Ait seulement su s'il avait un nom...
Dans le désert ainsi passe et s'écoule
Le filet d'eau modeste et sans renom...

Le voyageur s'est rafraîchi peut-être
A cette source errante, au fond des bois;
Mais pourrait-il encor la reconnaître
S'il la voyait une seconde fois?...

O pauvre! va... l'Eternelle Justice
Sait mieux que nous le pourquoi d'ici-bas...
La vie est courte et court le sacrifice;
Le monde est vil: ne le regrette pas!

Ah! si tes yeux avaient une étincelle
Qui pût encor regarder un moment,
Tu sourirais: car un ami fidèle
Derrière toi s'avance tristement...

Ton pauvre chien! l'enfant de ta misère,
La tête basse et les yeux abattus,
Malgré le froid, à ta halte dernière
Te suit encor, quand déjà tu n'es plus!

Quand tu seras dans la fosse commune,
Non loin de là, faible il se couchera;
Et puis bientôt quelque corbeau nocturne
Sur ses débris sanglants se perchera!

The Poor Man's Funeral Procession

For M. Emile Ribereau

Daylight grows dim beneath the icy rain;
The corpse-cart rolls in silence as the throng,
Over the dismal, darkening terrain,
Looks aside and goes hurrying along...

Who is that, on his voyage, all alone?
Whom does that wagon, somber-hued, escort?
His name? Doubtless some nobody, unknown,
Whose woes the Everlasting has cut short...

And so he passes by, and never could
The crowd know if he had a name at all...
Like modest brooklet, in the barren wood,
Trickling past, to its fate beyond recall...

Perhaps the thirsting woodland voyager
Sips a refreshing draught from it, and then
Walks on; but would he know it if he were
Ever, perchance, to see it yet again?

Poor soul!... Eternal Justice does the choosing
Here below: nor know we what it finds fit...
Life is short; short, the moment of its losing;
But vile, the world: mourn not the loss of it!

Ah! If your eyes had but one moment's spark
To let you look once more before the end,
How you would smile to see there, in the dark,
Trailing behind, sadly, one faithful friend...

Your poor dog! Offspring of your poverty,
With downcast eyes, head hanging low, heartsore...
Despite the cold, on this, your last ride, he
Follows you still, though now you are no more!

When you in paupers' common grave are laid,
Close will he lie, weak, but forever searching...
Soon, some night crow will, on his flesh decayed
And bloodied bones, come by and light, a-perching...

215

Toi

Tu ne murmuras point quand l'heure était venue,
    L'heure de nos adieux...
Tu t'envolas tranquille à travers chaque nue,
    Comme un ange des cieux.

Enfant, nous te suivrons au delà des nuages,
    Où l'âme trouve un port,
Où l'on n'entend jamais le grand bruit des orages,
    Où l'ouragan s'endort!

Camille Thierry (1814–75)

Camille Thierry was born in New Orleans in October of 1814 to Jean Baptiste Thierry, a Frenchman and editor of the *New Orleans Courrier de la Louisiane,* and a free woman of color. Thierry's mother had given birth to another figure well-known among the Creoles of color, the teacher and writer Michel Seligny. (Seligny founded the Sainte-Barbe Academy in New Orleans, a school for the wealthier members of the community.) When Thierry left New Orleans for France he turned over the management of his estate to a broker who defrauded him. He was not, however, penniless when he died.

Camille Thierry contributed fourteen poems to *Les Cenelles,* and periodically his poetry would appear in the New Orleans journals *La Chronique de la Nouvelle-Orléans* and *L'Orléanais.* Critics have long argued that Camille Thierry's poems are the best in *Les Cenelles.* They are certainly among the best of Louisiana's francophone poetry. In its unpretentious simplicity, his poetry is fresh, graceful, lyrical, and varied, addressing themes as disparate as those in "The Incubus" and "An Old Mulatress's Lament." In 1874 Camille Thierry published a volume of poetry, *Les Vagabondes;* he died in Bordeaux one year later, in 1875.

You

When the time came, you muttered not a sound—
    The time for our goodbyes...
Calm, you flew off, like angel heaven-bound,
    Over the shrouded skies.

Follow I shall, child, past the clouds, to reach
    A port of soul's safekeeping,
Where never brawls the tempest's blare and screech,
    And hurricane lies sleeping.

En ce jour de malheur où ta joyeuse tête
      Se pencha pour mourir,
Ton nom seul nous resta... débris que la tempête
      Laissa pour l'avenir!

Ce nom!... il restera dans l'ombre de mon âme
      Jusqu'à mon dernier jour...
N'est-il pas le reflet d'une brûlante flamme
      Qui me couvrit d'amour?...

Ce nom, dans le calice où je bois la misère,
      Distille un peu de miel,
Ce nom, il est encore un parfum sur la terre...
      Quand la fleur est au ciel!...

Femme Déchue

J'étais pure à quinze ans!—A ma ville natale
      Je disais mes chansons;
Puis j'allais écouter le chant que la cigale
      Jette dans les buissons!...

Plus tard, un beau jeune homme aux paroles de flamme
      Vint me dire à genoux,
Qu'il voulait allumer le foyer de mon âme
      Avec des feux bien doux.

Je lui donnai ma vie encor demi-fermée,
      Et pleine de trésors;
A l'amant qui baisait ma robe parfumée
      Je livrai mon beau corps!...

Soupira-t-il longtemps le vainqueur de mes charmes?...
      Il fit mourir ses feux
Sans écouter ma voix, sans regarder les larmes
      Qui tombaient de mes yeux!...

Malgré mon déshonneur, je suis encore trop belle
      Pour quitter les plaisirs;
Il renaît en mon cœur quelque vive étincelle,
      Quelques brûlants désirs!...

That day of grief, when, once so pert, your head
      Drooped low in death... Ah me!
The storm spared but your name, last relic, spread
      Before posterity.

That name, till death, will fill my soul... That name
      Will light the gloom thereof:
Is it not still a flicker of that flame
      That covered me with love?

That name! It honeys yet this cup of woe
      That I, alas, drink dry.
That name! It wafts its scent on earth, although
      The flower dwells in the sky!...

Fallen Woman

Pure village maid—fifteen!—I used to sing;
      But soon, among the thickets,
Off I would go, at nature's beckoning,
      To listen to the crickets!...

In time, a fair young swain, aflame with passion,
      On bended knee, said he
Yearned—burned!—to fire my soul in gentle fashion,
      Tenderly, properly.

I gave the beau my life, still scarce full-bloomed:
      My body rife with treasure.
He kissed my gown, with fragrance sweet-perfumed,
      As I bowed to his pleasure!...

Long did he sigh, this captor of my beauty?
      Nay! Quenched his flame, he kept
His peace... Saw naught, heard naught, disdained his booty,
      Nor knew the tears I wept!...

Now, though dishonored, I am still too fair
      To bid my joys adieu:
A spark ignites my heart, and, burning there,
      Desire's flames rise anew!...

Je vois toujours flotter quelque chose, en mon rêve,
　　D'inconnu, d'éclatant;
Je ne puis demander, quand mon soleil se lève,
　　La grille d'un couvent!...

J'étais pure à quinze ans!—A ma ville natale
　　Je disais mes chansons;
Puis j'allais écouter le chant que la cigale
　　Jette dans les buissons!...

　　Lorsque mon bruyant équipage
　　Fait voltiger le coquillage
　　Semé dans les creux du chemin,
　　Lorsque mes chevaux, blancs d'écume,
　　Semblent se baigner dans la brume
　　Qui se lève avec le matin,
　　Vos femmes de moi sont jalouses!...
　　Vos créatures, vos épouses
　　Ne peuvent cacher sous leurs traits
　　Tout le dépit qui les dévore,
　　Lorsque à leurs yeux je laisse éclore
　　La richesse de mes attraits!
　　Oui, quand je fais danser ma joie,
　　Et qu'un long ruban se déploie
　　Sur mes cheveux à l'abandon,
　　J'entends s'élever un murmure,
　　J'entends les mots de "femme impure,"
　　Mais jamais le mot de "pardon!"...
　　Dans le silence ou le tumulte,
　　Toujours il me vient quelque insulte;
　　Toujours quelques bouches diront
　　Mes amours et mes nuits de veille...
　　Qu'importe,—la couleur vermeille
　　Ne peut plus me monter au front!

J'étais pure à quinze ans!—A ma ville natale
　　Je disais mes chansons;
Puis j'allais écouter le chant que la cigale
　　Jette dans les buissons!...

In dreams I see, sky-borne, I know not what—
      Vague, and yet bright… But wait!…
Ah no! When dawns my morning sun, I'll not
      Knock at the convent gate!…

Pure village maid—fifteen!—I used to sing;
      But soon, among the thickets,
Off I would go, at nature's beckoning,
      To listen to the crickets!…

      Today, I ride with much display
      In coach-and-four, raising a spray
      Of dust—shells strewn among the ruts;
      And, as my horses, frothing, bound
      Over the fog-enshrouded ground,
      And, as the carriage proudly struts
      Its way amid the mists that rise,
      Cloudlike, beneath the morning skies,
      Your women look on jealously—
      Your wives, your paramours… And, oh!
      How they would fain conceal the woe,
      The spite they feel at seeing me
      Blooming with wealth before their eye!
      But no! They cannot!… And, when my
      Joy dances free—free as my hair,
      Blown by the wind, unribboned—ah!
      I hear a muttered murmur: "Bah!…
      Woman impure!…" But would they dare
      Say "pardon"…? Nay! Naught do they now
      But scorn my loves, my nights unsleeping…
      What matters it?… No more goes creeping
      A blush to tint my tainted brow!…

Pure village maid—fifteen!—I used to sing;
      But soon, among the thickets,
Off I would go, at nature's beckoning,
      To listen to the crickets!…

Clair de la Lune

Pourquoi montrer ta face blême?
Lune, pourquoi briller ce soir?
Quand tu parais, l'enfant que j'aime
Craint toujours de se laisser voir.
Les blancs rayons de ta lumière
La montreraient sur mes genoux...
Et l'on irait dire à sa mère:
Votre fille a des rendez-vous.

Je pourrai presser son corsage,
Je pourrai toucher ses cheveux,
Si tu te mets dans le nuage
Qui traverse l'air pur des cieux.
Ne sois pas sourde à ma prière:
Cache-toi, lune, cache-toi!...
Elle aime la nuit, le mystère,
Quand son cœur la conduit vers moi!...

Je t'aurai dans ma poésie,
Je t'aurai dans son doux regard,
Si tu mets ta tête jolie
Dans l'enveloppe du brouillard.
Ta lumière encore étincelle
Sur le feuillage de nos bois...
Disparais; je l'entends; c'est elle
Des fleurs couvrent ses jolis doigts!

A Mon Américaine

Sous ta belle écharpe de soie
Lorsque ton corps frêle se ploie,
Je dis: "La sylphide des airs,
Que le souffle d'un rêve incline,
Peut-être a la taille moins fine
Que celle dont parlent mes vers!..."

Moonlight

Why show your pallid face tonight?
Why shine, O moon? When you appear,
The child I love fears lest your light
Let someone come and find her here;
Someone who, as with her I sit,
Will to her mother run, insisting—
Seeing her on my lap, bright-lit:
"Madame, your daughter goes a-trysting."

I will caress her breast's fair skin,
I will caress, no less, her hair,
If you conceal yourself within
That cloud spread on the skies' pure air.
Hear me, please; heed my prayer: go, hide,
O moon! I beg you hidden be!
When her heart draws her to my side,
How she loves night's dark mystery!

You shall be mine in verse; and, too,
You shall be mine in her sweet glance,
If only, my fair beauty, you
Wrap your face in the mists' expanse...
But no! You sparkle on and on,
Upon this wooded grove of ours.
I hear her... Lo! she comes... Begone!...
Ah, see?... 'Tis she, hands heaped with flowers!...

To My American Miss

When I see your slim body sway
Beneath your fine silk scarf, I say:
"The sylph borne on the air—a thing
Of grace, that dream's breath airily
Wafts to and fro—perchance may be
Less lithe than she whom now I sing!..."

Que ne puis-je, même à cette heure,
Te voir errer dans la demeure
Qu'habitaient les ducs féodaux!
Là tu ferais du moyen âge
Revivre encor la grande image,
Qui dort à l'ombre des châteaux!...

Mais non!—Que n'as-tu pour asile
Les plis du nuage mobile
Que dore un rayon du matin!
Là tu serais loin de ce monde
Où quelque épine vagabonde
Insulte à tes pieds de satin!

Puisque tu n'as rien de la terre,
Dis-moi, dis-moi, belle étrangère,
Dis-moi, n'es-tu pas la willis
Qui, dans ses formes vaporeuses,
Etouffe les âmes rêveuses
Là-bas, au bord des grands taillis?...

L'Incube

Je vais hâter ma mort!—Une voix de l'enfer
M'a dit "Meurs! ne crains pas la morsure du ver;
Tu renaîtras incube, et celle qui t'outrage
Subira, chaque soir, ta volupté de rage;
Chaque soir, tes soupirs, dans l'espace perdus,
De nul être jamais ne seront entendus;
Chaque soir, tes baisers, enfants nés du mystère,
Lui feront soupirer quelques mots de la terre;
Esprit voluptueux, chaque soir tu pourras
Sans trouble, sans danger, te pâmer dans ses bras!..."
Oui! l'espoir me sourit au delà de la tombe;
Femme, pour te punir, il faut que je succombe!...

Why loll you not about, fair belle,
Where feudal dukes were wont to dwell,
Before my eyes to come and go,
And bring once more that image, rife
With things medieval, back to life,
That sleeps at night by old *châteaux*!

But no!... Why then do you not take
Refuge deep in the clouds, where break
Morn's golden rays? What sweet retreat,
Far from this earth where some stray thorn,
Wandering free, leaves bruised and torn
The satin smoothness of your feet!

Tell me! Tell me, fair stranger, who
Have nothing of this world! Are you
Not one of those dire *willi*-sprites[a]
Who, vaporous of form, snuff out
Those faithless souls, musing about,
There, by the woods, some cursèd nights?...

a. The reference is to the Eastern European super-
stition that jilted women can return as vengeful
spirits—*wil(l)is*—who make their faithless lovers
dance themselves to death. The translation
attempts to explain it a little more clearly than
does the original.

The Incubus

I must make haste to end my days, for I
Hear a voice, straight from hell, commanding: "Die!
Fear not the vile worm's bite. For you shall be
Reborn an incubus; and, each night, she
Who now offends you shall suffer your lust,
Your fleshly rage: your sigh, lost in the dust
Of emptiness, each night, shall sound unheard;
And, each night, many a low-moaned, earthy word
Will your hot spirit-kisses, darkness-spawned,
Draw from her lips; and you, yearning beyond
Mere passion, shall, in your voluptuousness,
Swoon softly, safely in her arms." Ah, yes!

Incube insatiable, en mes brûlants transports,
Sur ta couche j'irai, pour fatiguer ton corps,
L'étreindre, l'épuiser, et lorsqu'il sera grêle,
Qu'il n'aura plus de chair... ton époux, infidèle
A ses serments, fuira, tout pâle de frayeur,
Le chevet nuptial, en s'écriant: Horreur!!!...
Mais moi j'y resterai, j'y resterai sans crainte,
Car j'aime un cœur souffrant qui laisse aller sa plainte,
Une femme qui n'a pour charmes que des os,
A qui le malotru jette un sale propos;
Car j'aime, en ma débauche, un estomac qui râle,
Une voix qui s'éteint, une voix sépulcrale;
Car j'aime que la mort, pour le hideux tombeau,
N'arrache qu'un squelette à mes mains de bourreau!...

A Ma Muse

Muse chérie,
Parle à l'enfant
Qui dans la vie
Marche en riant;
Las du voyage,
Je veux prier
Et m'appuyer
Sur son corsage.
Sans l'effrayer,
Dis-lui que folle
Elle sera,
Que ma parole
La guérira;
Car, sur mon âme,
Je sais guérir
La jeune femme
Qui dans ma flamme
Jette un soupir.

Hope, madame, smiles at me beyond the tomb:
To do you in I must go meet my doom!...
I shall lie by your side, an incubus
Unsated; and I, in my ravenous,
Burning desire to lay your body low,
Shall, with my strength, clutch you, weaken you so,
That, when your flesh, at length, is all but gone;
When Monsieur looks, sees you so gaunt, so wan
And wizened, then he, ghastly pale with dread,
Forgetting all his vows, will flee your bed,
Crying: "Oh, horrors!..." I, however, will
Flee not, fearlessly, clinging faithful still.
I love the aching heart that groans its pains,
The woman, in her charms' rawboned remains,
Cursed by a boorish mate. In my debauch,
Oh, how I love to listen, keep my watch
Over her belly-rumblings, and rejoice
To hear her dim, dying, sepulchral voice,
And let my murderous hands, with her last breath,
Yield up a corpse, all bones, to hideous death!...

To My Muse

Sweet Muse, I pray
You go seek after
Her who, with laughter,
Wanders life's way;
Find her, and say
That, surfeited
With travel, I
Would rest my head,
Calm, by and by,
Tenderly pressed
Upon her breast
In gentle prayer;
That, should she be
Gone mad, I swear
One word from me
Will make her well;
For I can cure
The demoiselle

Pars! messagère
De mes amours;
Dis que pour plaire
J'ai mes beaux jours;
Ouvre ton aile;
Suis l'étincelle
D'un cœur aimant;
Mon âme est prête;
Va! ne t'arrête
Qu'en la voyant!...

Regrets d'une Vieille Mulâtresse; ou, Désespoir de Sanite Fouéron[a]

Miré! Quand mon té Saint-Domingue,
Négresses même té bijoux;
Blancs layo té semblé seringue,
Yo té collé derrière à nous.
     Dans yon ménage
     Jamain tapage,
L'amour yon blanc, c'était l'adoration!
     Yo pa té chiches,
     Yo té bien riches,
Yon bon bounda té vaut yon bitation!
   Temps-là changé, nous sur la paille,
   Nous que z'habitants té fêté...
   Avant longtemps yon blanc pété[a]
     Va hélé nous canaille!!!

---

a. This poem was set to the tune of "Qu'il va lentement
le navire," by Béranger.
b. Dénomination que les nègres donnaient aux petits blancs
(Moreau de Saint-Méry).

Whose sighs, for sure,
Fire my amour!
Muse-messenger,
Go! Speak to her;
Tell her my spring
Can please her yet.
Fly! Spread your wing;
From my soul, let
The spark of love
Lead you above,
Beside, behind her.
I know no peace:
So never cease
Until you find her!

An Old Mulatress's Lament;
or, Sanite Fouéron's Despair

Listen! Way back, Santo Domingo,
Black girls, them be like jewels! Just so!
White men, them pester us, them cling, oh!
Follow us everywhere we go.
Them live with us,
No fight, no fuss.
Love us like goddesses, worship, embrace!
Them never cheap,
Them pockets, deep:
Give what men want, them give us run of place!...
Time change, us poor. Now, you know what?
Before, them treat us fine, each one...
Soon, white brat laugh at us, make fun,
Go call us trash and slut!

A Hermina[a]

Amour, écoute un amant qui t'implore,
O Cupidon, le plus puissant des dieux!
Fils de Vénus, daigne exaucer mes vœux;
Hélas! rends-moi la beauté que j'adore—
Lorsque mon cœur est consumé d'amour
Loin d'Hermina je n'ai plus de beau jour.

Adoucissez le chagrin qui m'oppresse,
Doux souvenirs de mon premier bonheur.
L'absence, hélas! qui cause mon malheur,
L'absence même a doublé ma tendresse—
Lorsque mon cœur est consumé d'amour
Loin d'Hermina je n'ai plus de beau jour.

Hélas! pour moi, dans mon inquiétude,
Tous les plaisirs sont d'ennuyeux tourmens.
Rien maintenant ne peut flatter mes sens.
Le monde entier est une solitude;
Lorsque mon cœur est consumé d'amour
Loin d'Hermina je n'ai plus de beau jour.

---

a. This poem was set to a "minstrel air."

Valcour

B. Valcour, a Creole of color, contributed eleven poems to *Les Cenelles*. Although there is a paucity of biographical information on Valcour, including what the *B* stands for, we do know that he was a student of Constant Lépouzé, a Frenchman who taught French and Latin and who translated several odes and satires of Horace. Valcour was an apt student, for his poetry includes references to Virgil, Horace, and Lamartine.

For Hermina

Love, listen to a lover's plaintive plea,
O Cupid, of the gods the mightiest,
Venus's son! Alas! Grant my request:
Pray give the beauty I adore to me!
When love consumes my heart, wears it away,
Far from Hermina, dark becomes my day.

Lighten the woe that weights me with its touch,
Sweet memories of my early happiness!
Absence—the source, alas, of my distress—
Absence but makes me love yet twice as much.
When love consumes my heart, wears it away,
Far from Hermina, dark becomes my day.

Alas! For me, in my dole and despair,
My pleasures all are torments now become.
Naught can allay my senses' martyrdom:
My world is barren grown, alone and bare.
When love consumes my heart, wears it away,
Far from Hermina, dark becomes my day.

Suggestions for Further Reading

Amelinckx, Frans. "La Littérature louisianaise au xix siècle." *Présence francophone* 43 (1993): 10–24.

Ancelet, Barry, and Mathé Allain. *Littérature française de la Louisiane.* Bedford, N.H.: National Materials Development Center for French, 1981.

Bell, Caryn Cossé. *Revolution, Romanticism, and the Afro-Creole Protest Tradition in Louisiana, 1718–1868.* Baton Rouge: Louisiana State University Press, 1997.

Blassingame, John. *Black New Orleans, 1860–1880.* Chicago: University of Chicago Press, 1973.

Caulfeild, Ruby Van Allen. *The French Literature of Louisiana.* New York: Institute of French Studies, Columbia University Press, 1929.

Coleman, Edward Maceo, ed. *Creole Voices: Poems in French by Free Men of Color: First Published in 1845.* Washington D.C.: Associated, 1945.

Desdunes, Rodolphe. *Our People and Our History.* Trans. and ed. Sister Dorothea Olga McCants. Baton Rouge: Louisiana State University Press, 1973.

Fabre, Michel. "The New Orleans Press and French-Language Literature by Creoles of Color." In *Multilingual America: Transnationalism, Ethnicity, and the Languages of American Literature,* ed. Werner Sollors, 29–49. New York: New York University Press, 1998.

———. "New Orleans Creole Expatriates in France: Romance and Reality." In *Creole: The History and Legacy of Louisana's Free People of Color,* ed. Sybil Kein, 179–95. Baton Rouge: Louisiana State University Press, 2000.

Fortier, Alcée. "French Literature in Louisiana." *PMLA* 2 (1886): 31–60.

———. *Louisiana Studies: Literature, Customs and Dialects, History and Education.* New Orleans: F. F. Hansell, 1894.

Fortier, Edouard. *Les Lettres françaises en Louisiane.* Québec: Imprimerie l'Action Sociale Limite, 1915.

Latortue, Régine, and Gleason R. W. Adams, eds. and trans. *Les Cenelles: A Collection* of Poems by Creole Writers of the Early Nineteenth Century, ed. Armand Lanusse. Boston: G. K. Hall, 1979.

Martin, Joan. "*Plaçage* and the Louisiana *Gens de Couleur Libres:* How Race and Sex Defined the Lifestyles of Free Women of Color." In *Creole: The History and Legacy of Louisiana's Free People of Color,* ed. Sybil Kein, 57–70. Baton Rouge: Louisiana State University Press, 2000.

Rankin, David. Introduction to *My Passage at the New Orleans Tribune,* by Jean-Charles Houzeau, trans. Gerard Denault. Baton Rouge: Louisiana State University Press, 1984.

Roussève, Charles Barthelemy. *The Negro in Louisiana: Aspects of His History and His Literature.* New Orleans: Xavier University Press, 1937.

Senter, Caroline. "Creole Poets on the Verge of a Nation." In *Creole: The History and Legacy of Louisiana's Free People of Color,* ed. Sybil Kein, 276–94. Baton Rouge: Louisiana State University Press, 2000.

St. Martin, Gérard, and Jacqueline Voorhies, eds. *Ecrits louisianais du dix-neuvième siècle.* Baton Rouge: Louisiana State University Press, 1979.

Tinker, Edward Laroque. *Les Ecrits de langue française en Louisiane au 19ème siècle.* Paris: Librairie Ancienne Honoré Champion, 1932.

——. *Bibliography of the French Newspapers and Periodicals of Louisiana.* Worcester, Mass.: American Antiquarian Society, 1933.

Viatte, Auguste. *Histoire littéraire de l'Amérique française des origines à 1950.* Paris: Presses Universitaires de France, 1954.

——. *Anthologie littéraire de l'Amérique francophone.* Québec: Sherbrooke University, 1971.

——. "Complément à la bibliographie louisianaise d'Edward Larocque Tinker." *Revue de Louisiane* 3, no. 2 (1974): 12–57.

NORMAN R. SHAPIRO, a professor of Romance languages and literatures at Wesleyan University, is a widely published, award-winning translator of French plays, poetry, and prose. His many works include *Négritude: Black Poetry from Africa and the Caribbean* (1970), *The Fabulists French: Verse Fables of Nine Centuries* (1992), several volumes of the fables and tales of La Fontaine, and translations of Victor Séjour's plays *Diégarias* (*The Jew of Seville* [2002]) and *La Tireuse de cartes* (*The Fortune-Teller* [2002]).

M. LYNN WEISS is an associate professor of American studies at the College of William and Mary and the author of *Gertrude Stein and Richard Wright: The Poetics and Politics of Modernism* (1998), as well as introductions to Norman R. Shapiro's translations of Victor Séjour's plays *Diégarias* (*The Jew of Seville* [2002]) and *La Tireuse de cartes* (*The Fortune-Teller* [2002]).

WERNER SOLLORS, the Henry B. and Anne M. Cahot Professor of English literature and a professor of comparative and African American literature at Harvard University, is the cofounder and director of the Longfellow Institute, which is devoted to collecting and preserving American literature written in non-English languages. His many books include *Neither Black nor White yet Both: Thematic Explorations of Interracial Literature* (1997).

SECOND LINE PRESS
LOUISIANA HERITAGE SERIES

Creole Echoes: The Francophone Poetry of Nineteenth-Century Louisiana
Translated by Norman R. Shapiro. Introduction and notes by
M. Lynn Weiss.

Crescent Carnival by Francis Parkinson Keyes

Dinner at Antoine's by Francis Parkinson Keyes

The Fortune-Teller by Victor Séjour. (forthcoming)
Translated by Norman R. Shapiro.
Introduction by M. Lynn Weiss.

The Jew of Seville by Victor Séjour. (forthcoming)
Translated by Norman R. Shapiro.
Introduction by M. Lynn Weiss.

Jules Choppin: New Orleans Poems in Creole and French
Translated by Norman R. Shapiro.
Introduction by M. Lynn Weiss.

The River Road by Francis Parkinson Keyes

Steamboat Gothic by Francis Parkinson Keyes (forthcoming)

second
line
press

New Orleans, LA

Originally composed in 11/13 Bulmer with Cochin display
by Barbara Evans at the University of Illinois Press
Designed by Copenhaver Cumpston
Reprinted with adjustments by Black Widow Press